PEACEFUL
LONDON

Over 250 places to revive your spirits

David Hampshire

City Books • Bath • England

First published 2014 (as 'London's Secrets: Peaceful Places')
Second edition 2019

Copyright © City Books 2019
Cover Photo: Pergola, Hill Garden © I-Wei Huang (Adobe Stock)
Cover Design: Herring Bone Design

City Books, c/o Survival Books Limited
Office 169, 3 Edgar Buildings
George Street, Bath BA1 2FJ, United Kingdom
+44 (0)1305-266918, info@survivalbooks.net
citybooks.co, survivalbooks.net and londons-secrets.com

British Library Cataloging in Publication Data
A CIP record for this book is available
from the British Library.
ISBN: 978-1-909282-84-1

Printed in China

Acknowledgements

The author would like to thank all the many people who helped with research and provided information for this book. Special thanks are due to Gwen Simmonds for her invaluable research, Graeme & Louise Chesters and Richard Todd; Robbi Atilgan for editing; Susan Griffith for final proof checking; John Marshall for desktop publishing and photo selection; David Gillingwater for cover design; and the author's partner (Alexandra) for the constant supply of tea and coffee. Last, but not least, a special thank you to the many photographers – the unsung heroes – whose beautiful images bring London to life.

The Author

David Hampshire's career has taken him around the world and he lived and worked in many countries before taking up writing full-time. He's the author, co-author or editor of over 25 titles, including *London's Secret Places, London's Secrets: Museums & Galleries, London's Secrets: Parks & Gardens, London's Green Walks, London's Village Walks* and *London's Monumental Walks.* David was born in Surrey and lived and worked in London for many years and still considers himself a Londoner. Nowadays he divides his time between London and Dorchester (Dorset).

The Publisher

City Books is an imprint of Survival Books, which was established in 1987 and by the mid-1990s was the leading publisher of books for expats and migrants planning to live, work, buy property and retire abroad. In 2000, we published the first of our London books, *Living and Working in London*, and since then have added over 20 more London titles, including our new series of walks' books. We now specialise in alternative London guidebooks for both residents and visitors. See our websites for our latest titles.

Readers' Guide

♦ **Contact details:** These include the address, telephone number and website. You can enter the postcode to display a map of the location on Google and other map sites or, if you're driving, enter the postcode into your satnav.

♦ **Opening hours:** These can change at short notice, therefore you should confirm by telephone or check the website before travelling, particularly over Christmas/New Year and on bank holidays, when many places are closed. Many venues open daily, while some open only on weekdays. Note that some establishments – such as libraries – require visitors to register or to be a member (which may be free).

♦ **Transport:** The nearest tube or railway station is listed, although in some cases it may involve a lengthy walk. You can also travel to most venues by bus and to some by river ferry. Venues outside central London are usually best reached by car, although parking can be difficult or impossible in some areas. Most venues don't provide parking, particularly in central London, and even parking nearby can be a problem (and very expensive). If you need to travel by car, check the local parking facilities beforehand (or take a taxi).

♦ **Prices:** Prices are liable to change and are intended only as a guide. Many venues – such as museums, galleries, parks, gardens and places of worship – usually offer free entry. Where applicable, a price guide is shown as follows: £ = (relatively) inexpensive, ££ = moderate, £££ = expensive.

Disabled Access

Many historic public and private buildings don't provide wheelchair access or provide wheelchair access to the ground floor only. Wheelchairs are provided at some venues, although users may need assistance. Most museums, galleries and public buildings have a WC, although it may not be wheelchair accessible. Contact venues directly if you have specific requirements. The Disabled Go website (disabledgo.com) provides more in-depth access information for some destinations.

Contents

Kyoto Garden, Holland Park

Introduction

London is one of the world's most exciting cities, but it's also one of the noisiest; a bustling, chaotic, frenetic, over-crowded, manic metropolis of over 8 million people, where it can be difficult to find somewhere to grab a little peace and quiet. Nevertheless, if you know where to look London has a wealth of peaceful places – places to relax, chill out, contemplate, meditate, sit, reflect, browse, read, chat, nap, walk, think, study or even work (if you must) – where the city's volume is muted or even switched off completely.

Peaceful London contains over 250 of the author's and his friends', colleagues' and acquaintances' favourite locations throughout the city, from restful gardens and serene churches to silent libraries and inspiring galleries; intimate hotels to blissful spas and cosy cafés; interesting shops and atmospheric markets to appealing restaurants and charming tea rooms; quiet museums and lovely parks to relaxing neighbourhoods and friendly pubs – and much more. Moreover, these places haven't just been selected for their quietude but also for their excellence: every entry has something special to offer, be it a warm welcome, excellent food/drink, fascinating history, attractive ambience, glorious scenery or tempting wares on offer.

Peace is a relative term, however, and not all places are whisper-quiet all the time; even churches have bell-ringing and organ practice, and many parks host noisy school parties and sports events. You can, of course, expect bookshops, libraries, galleries, museums and spas (and churches and gardens!) to be peaceful most of the time, but even cafés, restaurants, pubs and bars can be surprisingly quiet – although you may need to time your visit a little more carefully. With regard to the latter, we have chosen venues with gardens, terraces, panoramic views and cosy corners – places where you can find a bit of personal space and grab some 'me' time along with your refreshments.

So, whether you're seeking a place to recharge your batteries, rest your head, revive your spirits, restock your larder or refuel your body; somewhere to inspire, soothe or uplift your mood; or just wish to discover a part of London that's a few steps further off the beaten track, *Peaceful London* will steer you in the right direction.

Silence is Golden!

David Hampshire
January 2019

1.
Afternoon Tea

There are few experiences more relaxing than the typically English ode to self-indulgence: afternoon tea. From the clink of silver on china to the soft sighs as you succumb to yet another tasty morsel, it's a supremely soothing way to while away a few hours. This chapter also offers some suggestions that take the experience well beyond just a few scones and cucumber sandwiches. See page 4 for a price guide.

Baskervilles Tea Shop

A lovely, old-fashioned teashop overlooking Broomfield Park in Palmers Green (north London), Baskervilles is passionate about the quality of its teas and the deliciousness of its scones and cakes. There's a wide range of teas, each blended to the shop's specification, including black, green and white teas to suit every mood and occasion.

Afternoon tea – which, weather permitting, can be enjoyed in the beautiful tranquil garden – features perennial favourites such as Victoria sponge, scones with clotted cream, cupcakes, lemon drizzle and chocolate brownies, plus a selection of dairy-, gluten- and wheat-free cakes. You can also buy teas to brew at home.

Baskervilles Tea Shop, 66 Alderman's Hill, N13 4PP (020-8351 1673; baskervillesteashop.co.uk; Palmers Green rail; Mon-Sat 9am-5.30pm, Sun 10am-5pm; £).

Brigit's Bakery

Situated in the heart of Covent Garden, Brigit's Bakery (or B Bakery for short) is the brainchild of French couple Philippe and Brigitte Bloch, who opened their authentic boutique bakery and patisserie (check out the fabulous cake counter) and *salon de thé* in 2012.

The scrumptious afternoon tea – a combination of English tradition with a delicate French twist – is served in their delightful pastel-painted tearoom. It includes a selection of sandwiches and cakes – macaroons, meringues, petits choux, mini cupcakes, blinis and quiches – and a huge choice of loose-leaf teas from French tea specialists Betjeman & Barton. There's the option to add Prosecco, Champagne or cocktails, and they even offer afternoon tea tours aboard a 1960 Routemaster bus!

Brigit's Bakery, 6-7 Chandos Place, WC2N 4HU (020-3026 1188; london.b-bakery.com/afternoon-tea-london; Leicester Square tube; Mon-Fri, Sun 10am-7pm, Sat 9am-8pm; ££).

Brown's Hotel

One of London's most elegant hotels, historic Brown's is where Queen Victoria used to take tea. The English Tea Room remains one of London's most fashionable venues, combining period features – wood panelling, open fires and intricate Jacobean ceilings – with comfortable sofas and armchairs, against a background of soft piano music.

The traditional afternoon tea (with optional Champagne) is superb and for the health-conscious there's a 'tea-tox' healthy option that's a lighter take on this timeless treat, with fewer carbs, less fat and dairy/gluten-free choices. It's somewhere to celebrate a special occasion with a special person.

Brown's Hotel, Albemarle Street, W1S 4BP (020-7518 4155; roccofortehotels.com/hotels-and-resorts/browns-hotel/restaurants-and-bars/english-tea-room; Green Park tube; daily noon-6.30pm; £££).

Dominique Ansel Bakery

Enjoy an extra special tea, on a beautiful covered garden terrace, created by the best pastry chef on the planet. This accolade was awarded to Dominique Ansel by The World's 50 Best Restaurants (theworlds50best.com), and his tea menu lives up to his reputation. It traces the path of a flower from seed to full bloom, featuring savoury and sweet bites, warm scones with homemade berry jam, clotted cream and more.

Choose from a trio of different menu options, from Signature afternoon tea to Sparkling tea with a glass of wine or bubbly, or Dominique's pièce de résistance, Splendid Tea, with special additions such as butter-poached Canadian lobster rolls and Sevruga caviar with buckwheat blinis and crème fraîche. Magnifique!

Dominique Ansel Bakery London, 17-21 Elizabeth Street, SW1W 9RP (020-7324 7705; dominiqueansellondon.com; Victoria tube/rail; Thu-Sun noon-4pm; £££).

Fortnum & Mason

A world-famous food emporium in Piccadilly, Fortnum & Mason (est. 1707) is a combination of delicatessen, department store, restaurant and living museum. Tea is served in the elegant green and blue Diamond Jubilee Tea Salon (opened by HM The Queen in 2012), where a pianist plays soothing tunes.

Fortnum's takes its tea *very* seriously – they offer some 80 varieties – and have expert 'tearistas' (a tea barista) on hand to advise and offer a complimentary tea-tasting session before you order. The beautiful table settings, with silver tea strainers and trademark duck-egg blue porcelain, are more than matched by the delectable food, which includes finger sandwiches, cakes (the chocolate and cherry is heavenly), pastries and scones. A national treasure and an unforgettable tea.

Fortnum & Mason, 181 Piccadilly, W1A 1ER (020-7734 8040; fortnumandmason.com/restaurants/afternoon-tea; Green Park/Piccadilly tube; Mon-Sat 11.30am-7/7.30pm, Sun 11.30am-5.45pm; £££).

The Langham

Claimed to be the birthplace of afternoon tea, the glorious Palm Court at the Langham has been serving tea to the cream of London society for over 150 years. The beautiful Palm Court evokes all the elegance and gentility (with obligatory tinkling piano) that you'd expect from the five-star Langham hotel.

Created by Cherish Finden – multi award-winning executive pastry chef – the Wedgwood Afternoon Tea is a bespoke version of the traditional tea, inspired by Wedgwood porcelain and served in tailor-made 'Langham Rose' Wedgwood teaware. It includes a selection of some 40 tea blends, beautiful cakes and pastries, scrumptious scones and delicate finger sandwiches. Plus Champagne if you wish!

The Langham, 1C Portland Place, Regent Street, W1B 1JA (020-7636 1000; langhamhotels.com/en/the-langham/london/dining/palm-court; Oxford Circus tube; daily noon-5.30pm; £££).

Mo Café

Mo Café is a division of the acclaimed Momo restaurant, a modern Moroccan souk-like restaurant offering superb North African cooking and one of London's most exotic interiors. The café specialises in Moroccan afternoon tea, served on the lovely terrace or in the chic café next to the main restaurant.

Tea consists of a substantial selection of savoury delights, such as Moroccan chicken wrap filled with a classic Moroccan chermoula (garlic and herb paste), cheese briouats (deep-fried puff pastries), and zaalouk and mechouia (smoked aubergine and roast peppers) served on toast. Mouth-watering sweets include *Maghrebi pastries* filled with dates, almonds and sesame, and scones with fig jam and clotted cream. Accompanied by a tempting selection of spicy Moroccan mint teas.

Mo Café, 25 Heddon Street, W1B 4BH (020-7434 4040; momoresto.com; Oxford/Piccadilly Circus tube; daily noon-4.30pm; £-££).

Newens The Original Maids of Honour

A stone's throw from the gates of Kew Gardens, Newens (est. 1850) is a charming traditional tea room and bakery steeped in history. Quintessentially English, it's named after a melt-in-the-mouth cake that allegedly took Henry VIII's fancy when he found Anne Boleyn and the other Maids of Honour scoffing them at Richmond Palace. The recipe is a well-kept secret to this day, but they appear to have a puff pastry base, a layer of curd and a topping of (cheddar?) cheese – delicious and very moreish.

The tea room offers a variety of set teas ranging from a simple cream tea through a range of afternoon teas (with a choice of cake) and high tea (with sandwiches and savoury options as well). The pièce de résistance is, of course, Champagne high tea.

Newens The Original Maids of Honour, 288 Kew Road, TW9 3DU (020-8940 2752; theoriginalmaidsofhonour.co.uk; Kew Gardens tube; daily 8.30am-5.30pm; £-££).

Orange Pekoe

Award-winning Orange Pekoe (est. 2006) is a temple to tea, offering loose leaf teas in their purest form – indeed owners Marianna and Achilleas travel far and wide to find the finest handpicked tea leaves in the world. The tearoom is named after a tea grading term that refers to a range of high grade black teas of differing qualities and sizes, grown in India, Nepal and especially Sri Lanka (Ceylon).

Afternoon tea at OP is an informal affair and features the classic all-day cream tea of scones served with Cornish clotted cream and strawberry preserve, or traditional afternoon tea with sandwiches and cake. But it's the tea that takes centre stage and all 60 or so loose leaf or flower teas can be purchased in beautiful tea caddies or refill pouches.

Orange Pekoe, 3 White Hart Lane, SW13 0PX (020-8876 6070; orangepekoeteas.com; Barnes Bridge rail; daily 2-5pm; £-££).

The OXO Tower Brasserie

The OXO Tower is a landmark building in Southwark on the south bank of the Thames, acquired by the manufacturers of OXO beef stock cubes and largely rebuilt to an Art Deco design in the 1920s. It was refurbished in the '90s, with

the OXO Tower restaurant, bar and brasserie on the rooftop.

The Brasserie is operated by Harvey Nichols and offers afternoon tea with a difference – the difference being that 'tea' consists of four dessert tasting plates on a theme, e.g. Autumn or Foraging, teamed with a matching bespoke cocktail or Champagne. A little confusingly it's called 'Not Afternoon Tea'. A range of other equally original 'tea experiences' is available, too. An adventure for the tastebuds to rival Willy Wonka's creations – with views to die for!

The OXO Tower Brasserie, OXO Tower Wharf, Barge House Street, SE1 9PH (020-7803 3888; harveynichols.com/restaurants/oxo-tower-london; Waterloo rail/tube; Sun-Fri 3-5pm, Sat 2-4.30pm; ££-£££).

The Ritz

Served since 1906, afternoon tea at The Ritz is regarded by many as the quintessential English tea 'ceremony'. It's impeccably served in the spectacular Palm Court – originally called the Winter Garden – a dramatic, elegant salon of fanciful design, flanked by walls of mirrors, a ceiling of intricate gilded trellis design, marble pillars, birdcage chandeliers with ornate metal flowers, a striking stone fountain with gilded statues, fronded palms and a stunning central floral display.

Tea at The Ritz is formal and theatrical, as you take your place on the Palm Court's 'stage', populated by elegantly-dress guests and immaculate waiters flitting among the tables set with delicate fine bone china and gleaming silver tea services, against a backdrop of soothing music from the resident pianist or string quartet.

The menu follows the classic theme: a selection of around 18 loose-leaf teas; delicate finger sandwiches with traditional fillings such as smoked salmon, cucumber, egg, roast ham and cheese; a daily selection of scrumptious tea cakes and pastries; and freshly-baked raisin and apple scones with strawberry preserve and Cornish clotted cream. For a special occasion you can order the celebration tea, which includes a celebratory cake. One for the bucket list but remember to book well in advance.

The Ritz, 150 Piccadilly, W1J 9BR (020-7300 2345; theritzlondon.com/palm-court; Green Park tube; daily 11.30am-9pm; £££).

The Shard

Afternoon tea at the Shard – the tallest building in Europe – gives a whole new meaning to the term 'high tea'. Three Shard restaurants offer a tea service, all offering breath-taking views of the city's skyline.

Aqua Shard (020-3011 1256, daily 1-5pm, £££) offers a contemporary English afternoon tea with a modern twist, served in the restaurant's atrium located on the 31st floor. Tea includes delicious finger sandwiches such as Earl Grey tea-smoked Loch Duart salmon with caviar and dill-scented cream, while sweet delights include lemon meringue tart and cassis and yoghurt panna cotta.

One floor up, London Afternoon Tea at **Oblix West** (020-7268 6700, daily 2.45-4.30pm, £££) presents the very best produce from the capital, be it chai spices from Brick Lane or honeycomb from Harrow. The menu includes delicious sandwiches such as duck egg and truffle mayonnaise, scrumptious scones (cranberry, fresh honeycomb) and decadent pastries (yuzu and grapefruit,

pistachio and cherry). The choice of teas includes white peony, Cornish manuka and hibiscus flowers.

Higher still, the contemporary, Chinese-style **Ting Lounge at Shangri-La** (020-7234 8108, Mon-Sat noon-4pm, Sun noon-6pm, £££) on the 35th floor offers Traditional Afternoon Tea with a fine selection of sandwiches and desserts (such as cherry blossom roulade and lemon lavender tart), plus a choice of over 30 teas and optional Champagne.

Tea at the Shard isn't cheap, but is well worth it for the amazing panoramic views – and it saves you paying a hefty fee (over £30 for an adult) simply to visit the viewing platform!

The Shard, 32 London Bridge Street, SE1 9SG (the-shard. com/restaurants; London Bridge tube/rail; £££).

Sketch

If you want afternoon tea with a wow factor, Michelin-starred Sketch is hard to beat. A fashionable venue for food, art and music, it has a traditional but innovative afternoon tea menu created by chef Pierre Gagnaire. Tea is served in two very different rooms: the Glade, a fairy-tale dining room featuring ethereal woodland murals and wicker furnishings, and the Gallery, a breath-taking boudoir in stunning pink velvet designed by India Mahdavi, with provocative art by David Shrigley.

The tea itself – with optional (and irresistible) Champagne – offers a choice of around 20 teas (by Jing) and a show-stopping assortment of sweet and savoury treats: raspberry meringues, bubble gum marshmallows, dainty macaroons decorated with rose petals, caviar and quail's egg sandwiches, to mention just a few. Don't forget to visit the stunning egg-pod loos!

Sketch, 9 Conduit Street, W1S 2XG (020-7659 4500; sketch. london; Oxford Circus tube; daily 11.30-4pm; £££).

Teanamu Chaya Teahouse

Teanamu Chaya Teahouse offers a unique afternoon tea with an Asian twist in a serene and calm hideaway off bustling Portobello Road. Entering tea master Pei Wang's quaint teahouse is to be instantly soothed, where 'taking tea' is an intimate and ceremonial experience – and a much healthier one than the sugar-laden traditional English treat.

Savour elegant open sandwiches, delicate, handmade patisserie and Chinese dim sum, such as kumquat ginger preserve and mature cheddar on wakame seaweed brown bread, vegetarian dumplings with chilli oil; mango seed cake and peanut sesame cookies; and olive oil lemon cake with mango curd. All accompanied by a choice of elegant, handmade Chinese and Japanese teas.

Teanamu Chaya Teahouse, 4 Melina Road, W12 9HZ (teanamu.com/teahouse; Goldhawk Road tube; Sat-Sun noon-6pm; £-££).

The Wolseley

Tea consists of lavish stacks of finger sandwiches, fruit scones and a selection of scrumptious cakes such as Battenberg or Sachertorte, accompanied by a pot of tea of your choice (although not as extensive as some other establishments) and optional Champagne. Nice touches are the hourglass timer (to time your tea), silver tea strainers and luxurious linen napkins. Those wanting a lighter option can choose the cream tea. Go for the ambience and the fascinating people-watching.

The Wolseley, 160 Piccadilly, W1J 9EB (020-7499 6996; thewolseley.com/afternoon-tea; Green Park tube; Mon-Fri 3-6.30pm, Sat-Sun 3.30-6.30pm; £-££).

The Wolseley is an elegant café-restaurant in the grand European tradition, occupying the former car showroom of Wolseley Motors designed in the '20s by William Curtis Green. The architect drew on Venetian and Florentine influences with exotic Eastern touches to create a majestic interior with marble floors, towering Corinthian pillars, grand arches and sweeping stairways – it's one of London's most beautiful and atmospheric spaces.

Afternoon tea is served in the cosy café, where there's a more casual atmosphere, although service is as polished as in the main dining room. It effortlessly blends English tradition with the quintessential European feel of the restaurant, and manages to offer a more modern (and less expensive) alternative to its chintzy neighbour, The Ritz.

2.
Bookshops

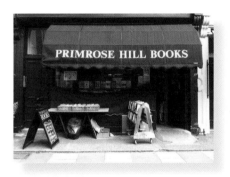

Bookshops are one of the few places where you can browse at length without attracting the attention of an over-enthusiastic salesperson – where, indeed, you're positively encouraged to linger at your leisure. London has some of the best in the world, from general book stores to antiquarian, specialist to secondhand, offering seats and quiet corners, often with a cosy café for good measure.

Daunt Books

Founded in 1990 by James Daunt, the chain's flagship store on Marylebone High Street is housed in a beautiful Edwardian bookshop dating from 1912, believed to be the first custom-built bookshop in the world. The back room is particularly impressive, with its original oak mezzanine gallery, graceful skylights and stained-glass window. Entering the bookshop is like rewinding to a calmer, more graceful era, when people had time to browse and customer service wasn't just a cliché – staff are knowledgeable, while the books are beautifully displayed.

Although it isn't a travel bookshop, Daunt is seen first and foremost as a travel specialist thanks to its elegant three-level back room, home to row upon row of guide books, maps, language reference books, history, politics, travelogues and related fiction. It's also good for literary fiction, biography, gardening and much more, and stages regular talks and events (see website for details).

Daunt Books has been trading for almost 30 years – a relatively short time in the book world – and now operates six shops (plus another three independent outlets) and has an enviable reputation as one of London's most popular independent booksellers. Daunt also branched out into publishing in 2010.

Daunt Books, 83 Marylebone High Street, W1U 4QW (020-7224 2295; dauntbooks.co.uk; Baker Street tube; Mon-Sat 9am-7.30pm, Sun 11am-6pm).

Dulwich Books

for young children. It stocks greetings cards, gift stationery/wrap, magazines, literary journals, notebooks, diaries and calendars, plus a range of educational games for children. The shop also offers eBooks via its website and in store.

You can sign up to the bookshop's email newsletter via their excellent website, but don't let that stop you paying a visit and exploring delightful Dulwich Village at the same time. It's a fitting destination for bibliophiles as it's also home to another award-winning bookshop, Village Books.

Dulwich Books, 6 Croxted Road, West Dulwich, SE21 8SW (020-8670 1920; dulwichbooks.co.uk; West Dulwich rail; Mon-Sat 9.30am-5.30pm, Sun 11am-4pm).

This West Dulwich bookshop celebrated its 35th anniversary in 2018 and has been lauded as one of Britain's best. Indeed, *The Bookseller* trade magazine voted Dulwich Books London's Best Independent Bookshop in 2012 and 2013, and the UK & Ireland Best Independent Bookshop in 2014. It's now owned by one of its most loyal customers, Susie Nicklin, who purchased the shop in 2015.

Dulwich Books stocks over 8,500 titles – children's and adults' books, fiction and non-fiction – and specialises in providing personal recommendations. It's very much a community bookshop, engaging closely with authors, customers, schools and colleges. One of the secrets of the shop's success is its comprehensive programme of readings and signings – attracting a plethora of celebrity authors – including readings

The European Bookshop

Owned by the European Schoolbooks (ESB) group of Cheltenham, the European Bookshop – incorporating the Young Europeans Bookstore and Italian Bookshop – has been supplying expatriates, language students and others with foreign-language publications for over 40 years, and is widely recognised as one of the best foreign-language bookshops in the world. Everything in the ESB catalogue – the UK's leading specialist distributor, wholesaler and retailer of books in European languages other than English – is normally kept in stock at the bookshop, plus the latest continental literature, important language titles from UK publishers and a comprehensive children's section.

The European Bookshop, 123 Gloucester Road, SW7 4TE (020-7734 5259; europeanbookshop.com; Gloucester Road tube; Mon-Fri 9.30am-6.30pm, Sat 10am-6.30pm, Sun noon-5pm).

Foster Books

Established in 1968, this family-run bookshop occupies the oldest shop on Chiswick High Road, dating from the late 18th century and Grade II listed. It's now managed by (second generation) Stephen Foster, whose claims to fame include sourcing rare books for the film industry, including many James Bond movies. Foster specialise in antiquarian books, fine bindings, illustrated children's books and first editions, as well as general stock with subjects leaning towards literature and the arts. The shop is a booklover's dream with classic books overflowing from floor-to-ceiling shelves and piled high on every available surface, exuding the intoxicating aroma of old books. You can lose yourself in this little slice of book heaven.

Foster Books, 183 Chiswick High Road, W4 2DR (020-8995 2768; fosterbooks.co.uk; Turnham Green tube; Mon-Sat 10.30am-5.30pm, Sun 11am-5pm).

Gay's The Word

A much-loved community bookshop and the only surviving LGBT bookshop in the UK, GTW stocks a wide range of books ('from the profound to the frivolous'), including fiction, 'gay' theory, and titles covering more practical matters, such as how to tell your mother you're gay.

The shop was established in 1979, when gay books weren't generally available in ordinary bookstores, and is now a major supplier to libraries and resource centres across the UK and worldwide. It isn't just a place to buy books, but has become an important community hub, hosting regular discussion groups and meetings, supported by gay icons such as Sir Ian McKellen and Stephen Fry.

Gay's The Word, 66 Marchmont Street, WC1N 1AB (020-7278 7654; facebook.com/gaystheword; Russell Square tube; Mon-Sat 10am-6.30pm, Sun 2-6pm).

Hatchards

Hatchards is London's oldest bookshop and the second-oldest in the UK (after the Cambridge University Press bookshop). Founded in 1797 by John Hatchard on Piccadilly (opposite the Royal Academy) – from where it still trades today – it's also the city's most aristocratic bookshop. Past customers have included many of Britain's greatest royal, political, social and literary figures, from Queen Charlotte (it boasts three Royal Warrants), Disraeli and Gladstone, to Wellington, Kipling and Byron.

Hatchards is a heady mix of old-world character and personal service, and a favourite with writers and readers. As such, it has a stellar reputation for attracting famous authors for signings/readings, and its star guests have included JK Rowling, David Attenborough, Sebastian Faulks and Michael Palin among others.

Hatchards, 187 Piccadilly, W1J 9LE (020-7439 9921; hatchards.co.uk; Piccadilly Circus tube; Mon-Sat 9.30am-8pm, Sun noon-6.30pm).

Heywood Hill

Occupying two floors of a Georgian townhouse in the heart of Mayfair (opposite Shepherd Market), Heywood Hill has been supplying the worthy citizens of London with reading material since 1936. Today, it's owned by Peregrine 'Stoker' Cavendish, the 12th Duke of Devonshire, whose family have long been supporters of the shop. Selling new, old and antiquarian books, as well as producing catalogues on numerous themes, it specialises in literature, history, architecture, biography, travel and children's books.

The shop's staff are all dedicated bibliophiles who delight in matching books with customers – and vice versa. They go out of their way to learn their clients' reading tastes in order to offer a tailored literary service.

Heywood Hill, 10 Curzon Street, W1J 5HH (020-7629 0647; heywoodhill.com; Green Park tube; Mon-Fri 9.30am-6pm, closed Sat-Sun).

John Sandoe Books

John Sandoe opened his celebrated bookshop in 1957 (and sold it in 1989 to like-minded new owners), since when it has become a Chelsea institution. The handsome shop occupies three floors of a beautiful 18th-century building off the King's Road and, while it has moved with the times, it remains essentially the same: an independent literary bookshop. Space is limited, yet they still manage to shoehorn in some 25,000 books, packed from floor to ceiling, stacked up the stairs and piled on tables.

This isn't a shop in which to pick up the latest blockbuster, but rather an invaluable resource for professionals, a treasure trove for discerning readers and a delight for browsers. A visit to John Sandoe makes buying books the exciting experience it should be.

John Sandoe Books, 10 Blacklands Terrace, SW3 2SR (020-7589 9473; johnsandoe.com; Sloane Square tube; Mon-Sat 9.30am-6.30pm, Sun 11am-5pm).

Libreria

Founded in 2016 by tech entrepreneur Rohan Silva (as part of his Second Home workspace project), Libreria is intended as an antidote to the technological age; mobile phones are banned here. However, the dramatic design by Spanish architects SelgasCano – intended to mimic Argentinian author Jorge Luis Borges's short story, *The Library of Babel* – feels very 21st century with its mirrored ceiling and wall-to-wall curved bookshelves in startling yellow, designed by graduates of the Slade School of Fine Art.

Libreria is that rare bookshop that *isn't* also trying to be a cool coffee shop, vinyl store or hipster hangout. Chairs and intimate reading booths are plentiful, and the aim is to help visitors find books that they might not otherwise come across and to move readers away from the 'people who bought this also bought XYZ' banality that you find online.

Books are arranged into broad suggestive themes and genres like 'The City', 'Wanderlust' and 'Sea and the Sky', rather than traditional sections such as crime, romance and poetry, while more exotic themes include 'Enchantment for the Disenchanted' and 'Mothers, Madonnas and Whores', all designed to provoke browsers into making unexpected connections. Libreria stages a wide range of events and workshops, including the occasional all-nighter, and has a Risograph printer for creative copying. An absolute gem.

Libreria, 65 Hanbury Street, E1 5JP (libreria.io; Aldgate East tube/ Shoreditch High Street rail; Tue-Wed 10am-6pm, Thu-Sat 10am-8pm, Sun 11am-6pm, closed Mon).

London Review Bookshop

Owned by the celebrated literary journal, *London Review of Books* (lrb.co.uk), the London Review Bookshop opened in May 2003, a stone's throw from the British Museum in Bloomsbury. It's one of the city's most distinctive independent bookshops: an attractive space with a soothing ambience, stocking an eclectic, well-chosen range of books that can be browsed in peace and quiet.

The LRB stocks the widest array of books imaginable (general interest and scholarly tomes – no blockbusters here) within a space that's easy to navigate. The passionate and highly-knowledgeable staff really care about their stock and their customers. The bookshop also functions as a forum for literary presentations and intellectual exchanges through a series of readings, discussions and lectures that are always engaging and interesting. You can sign up to its newsletter on their excellent website.

However, the LRB is much more than 'just' a bookshop and also houses one of the city's most popular cafés: the London Review Cake Shop. This is a self-indulgent marriage of books, coffee and cake, serving such sweet editions as rose and pistachio cake and rich chocolate and Guinness cake. It's a fine example of how to turn a bookshop into a social hang out – a modern-day literary coffee house.

London Review Bookshop, 14-16 Bury Place, WC1A 2JL (020-7269 9030; londonreviewbookshop.co.uk; Holborn tube; Mon-Sat 10am-6.30pm, Sun noon-6pm).

Lutyens & Rubinstein

Founded in 2009 by literary agents Sarah Lutyens and Felicity Rubinstein, this beloved bijou bookshop is situated

opposite the Kitchen & Pantry coffee shop in Notting Hill. It's the perfect spot for some in-depth browsing for discerning readers – a companionable and idiosyncratic experience for those who love books. Browsing is actively encouraged, and there are places to sit and read without any pressure to buy, aided and abetted by a tiny 'coffee shop' downstairs. The stock (around 4,000 tomes – L&R rates quality over quantity) comprises a cleverly curated but expansive range of fiction, non-fiction, poetry, graphic novels, children's classics and coffee-table volumes, with the emphasis on writing excellence and narrative.

Lutyens & Rubinstein, 21 Kensington Park Road, W11 2EU (020-7229 1010; lutyensrubinstein.co.uk/bookshop; Ladbroke Grove tube; Mon, Sat 10am-6pm, Tue-Fri 10am-6.30pm, Sun 11am-5pm).

Maggs Bros. Ltd

Established in 1853, Maggs is one of the world's largest antiquarian booksellers and the Holy Grail for collectors of rare books. Its founder was Uriah Maggs (a Dickensian name, if ever there was one) who, at the age of 25, left his home town of Midsomer Norton in Somerset to set up business in London (in typically Dickensian fashion), and it's appropriately housed in a fine 18th-century townhouse in the heart of Mayfair. Maggs sells books and manuscripts of the highest quality and acts as an advisor and bookseller to many of the world's finest collections, both private and institutional, in addition to stocking more affordable books. Or, as the website puts it, Maggs is 'serious about books without being stuffy'.

Maggs Bros. Ltd, 46 Curzon Street, W1J 7UH (020-7493 7160; maggs.com; Green Park tube; Mon-Sat 10am-6pm, closed Sun).

Nomad Books

A lovely, welcoming bookshop on Fulham Road, Nomad Books (est. 1990) is bright and airy with wooden floors, comfy sofas and a café. The beautiful main room is packed with recommendations to inspire readers, while there's also a good children's section, gifts and stationery, and a regular book club. Nomad offers some clever ideas to challenge and inspire, including a 'reading clinic', whereby an advisor asks you about your likes and dislikes and, based on your answers, 'prescribes' six books for you to receive over the coming year. The shop can also advise on books to take with you when travelling, and designs book 'bundles' to give as gifts.

Nomad Books, 781 Fulham Road, SW6 5HA (020-7736 4000; nomadbooks.co.uk; Parsons Green tube; Mon-Sat 10am-6pm, Sun 11am-5pm).

Pages of Hackney

A bijou bookshop on Lower Clapton Road's 'murder mile' – it was the local post office until the postmaster was shot dead in a robbery – Pages of Hackney stocks an eclectic selection of contemporary and classic fiction for adults and children, plus travel, politics, environment, art, cookery and more. There's also a good second-hand section in the basement, full of Penguin classics and children's books. The shop was opened in 2008 by Eleanor Lowenhall, who lives upstairs, and quickly became a thriving community and cultural hub. Pages is a previous winner of the Mayor of Hackney's Business Awards' Best New Business and has also been shortlisted for *The Bookseller* Independent Bookseller of the Year. A classic community bookshop.

Pages of Hackney, 70 Lower Clapton Road, E5 0RN (020-8525 1452; pagesofhackney.co.uk; Hackney Downs rail; Mon-Fri 11am-7pm, Sat 10am-6pm, Sun 11am-6pm).

Primrose Hill Books

This wonderful little bookshop, owned and run by Jessica Graham and Marek Laskowski, has been a local landmark in Primrose Hill for over 25 years. Inside there's a well-chosen selection of titles, both hardback and paperback, bestsellers and reference books, travel guides and a good mystery section. There's also a good choice of children's books, including all the favourites, plus a selection of lesser-known titles discovered over the years. The shop specialises in rare and out-of-print books, and has an assortment of second-hand books. You may even spot one of the gilded Primrose Hill set while perusing the shelves…

Primrose Hill Books, 134 Regent's Park Road, NW1 8XL (020-7586 2022; primrosehillbooks.com; Chalk Farm tube; Mon-Fri 9.30am-6pm, Sat 10am-6pm, Sun 11am-6pm).

Skoob Books

An underground temple for used academic books, Skoob is home to over 55,000 works covering subjects that aren't often to be found in second-hand bookshops, from philosophy, maths and science to languages, literature and criticism, art and history to economics and politics. Stock is regularly refreshed by owner Chris Edwards from his Oxford warehouse where he has another million books! While it's located in a basement with concrete walls and exposed piping (and no windows), the shop is light and airy, with lift access, bespoke lighting, heating/air-conditioning and knowledgeable staff – all of which make for a rewarding browsing environment. There's a discount for students and 10 per cent off for Curzon cinema card holders, too.

Skoob Books, 66 The Brunswick, off Marchmont Street, WC1N 1AE (020-7278 8760; skoob.com; Russell Square tube; Mon-Sat 10.30am-8pm, Sun 10.30am-6pm).

Tales on Moon Lane

A recipient of numerous accolades, including twice 'Children's Bookshop of the Year' winner at *The Bookseller* Industry Awards, Tales on Moon Lane is an enchanting children's bookshop in Herne Hill, south London. Owned by Tamara Macfarlane, it specialises in books for children of all ages, from toddlers to teenagers, from classics such as Narnia and Beatrix Potter to contemporary giants like JK Rowling and Philip Pullman, and the best new children's authors. The shop is a magnet for children, with weekly storytelling sessions, phonics' workshops for toddlers, a dedicated kids' book group and half-term reading groups. It also arranges school visits by authors and illustrators and is a regular fixture at book fairs.

Tales on Moon Lane, 25 Half Moon Lane, SE24 9JU (020-7274 5759; talesonmoonlane.co.uk; Herne Hill rail; Mon-Sat 9am-5.30pm, Sun 10.30am-4.30pm).

Word on the Water

London's most unusual bookshop, Word on the Water is housed on a 100-year-old Dutch barge moored on the Regent's Canal towpath in King's Cross. Launched in 2010 by owners Paddy Screech and Jonathan Privett, this 'bookbarge' used to chug along the capital's waterways, relocating every fortnight (due to mooring regulations), and was threatened with closure in 2015. However, thanks to an enthusiastic petition, it was granted a permanent mooring alongside Granary Square and has now dropped anchor for good. Quirky and cosy (dog-friendly, too) – with a wood-burning stove in

winter – it offers a wide selection of 'interesting' new and second-hand books, including a large children's section. Happenings include 'meet the author' events, talks, and jazz and poetry nights on the roof 'stage'. Welcome aboard!

Word on the Water, Regent's Canal Towpath, Granary Square, N1C 4AA (07976-886982; facebook.com/wordonthewater; King's Cross/St Pancras tube/rail; daily noon-7pm).

3.
Cafés & Restaurants

Some cafés and restaurants are solely for sustenance, while others also feed your soul by providing somewhere you can enjoy some (relatively) undisturbed quality time. Those featured here offer delicious food and beverages but also something special, be it a charming building, a calming ambience or a lovely (often alfresco) space to retreat to. See page 4 for a price guide.

L'Absinthe

This pretty, traditional French bistro (plus cafe, deli and outside catering service) in Primrose Hill opened in 2007 and quickly became a favourite destination for the local community. Fronted by charming, friendly expat Burgundian and 'Grand Fromage' Jean-Christophe (JC) Slowik, L'Absinthe offers a bright and cosy dining room, conservatory and small courtyard. Here you can enjoy excellent French cooking such as classic fish soup with *rouille* and croutons, duck confit with braised red cabbage, and crème brûlée with blackcurrant sauce. While the breakfast/lunch menu offers treats like croques, crepes and pain perdu (French toast). There's a well-chosen (mostly French) wine list or you can bring your own. *Magnifique!*

L'Absinthe, 40 Chalcot Road, NW1 8LS (020-7483 4848; labsinthe.co.uk; Chalk Farm tube; Mon-Fri 8am-3pm, 6-10pm, Sat 9am-3pm, 6-10pm; French; £).

Bloomsbury Coffee House

A friendly café/coffee house in central Bloomsbury – voted Best Coffee Place in Bloomsbury, Fitzrovia and Holborn 2018 by *Time Out* – BCH is a cosy hangout in which to enjoy breakfast (organic full English and sourdough toast), fine coffee and a tasty brunch/lunch. Brunch is served until 11.30am weekdays (1.30pm weekends) and there's a changing daily lunch menu of savouries, salads and soups during the week, not forgetting their delicious freshly baked treats – with gluten-free

and vegan choices. The café has two rooms, plus a small courtyard for sunny days, and there are plenty of sockets and quiet spaces for those wishing to work/study, although weekends can be very busy.

Bloomsbury Coffee House, 20 Tavistock Place, WC1H 9RE (020-7837 2877; bloomsburycoffeehouse.co.uk; Russell Square tube; Mon-Fri 8am-6pm, Sat-Sun 8am-1.30pm; £).

Blueprint Café

Located on the first floor of the former Design Museum building in Bermondsey, the Blueprint Café (operated by D&D London) enjoys an enviable location on the south bank of the Thames, offering superb views of Tower Bridge, the City and Canary Wharf. It's the perfect setting to experience the innovative, seasonal British cuisine of chef-patron Mini Patel, whose menus have a particular focus on small plates with a playful and contemporary twist. There's a reasonable fixed-price menu including the likes of smoked haddock fishcakes, beef and coconut curry, and set lemon cream with blackberries and amaretti crumbs.

Blueprint Café, 28 Shad Thames, SE1 2YD (020-7378 7031; blueprintcafe.co.uk; Tower Hill/London Bridge tube; Tue-Fri noon-2.45pm, 5.30-10pm, Sat 11am-2.45pm, 5.30-10pm, Sun noon-3.45pm, closed Mon; British; £-££).

Brawn

One of London's best neighbourhood East End restaurants, Brawn is fully on-trend, from its chic industrial vibe – located in a former warehouse with high ceilings, whitewashed walls and concrete floors – to its excellent-value, seasonal, European-influenced menu. Dishes revolve around fashionable ingredients such as smoked eel, red mullet, burrata (Italian soft cheese) and rainbow chard, plus a tempting array of puddings, including such flavours as bergamot and lemon, and dark chocolate, olive oil and sea salt, accompanied by 'natural' (organic or biodynamic) wines sourced from sustainable small growers. On Sundays Brawn offers a fixed-price menu – a splendid treat after exploring the nearby flower market. Brawn is a delight.

Brawn, 49 Columbia Road, E2 7RG (020-7729 5692; brawn. co; Hoxton rail; Mon 4-10.30pm, Tue-Sat noon-3pm, 6-10.30/11pm, Sun noon-4pm; European; ££).

Buttery Café

Buttery Café, Burgh House, New End Square, NW3 1LT (020-7794 3943; burghhouse.org.uk/visit/buttery-cafe; Hampstead tube; Wed-Fri 10am-5pm, Sat-Sun 9.30am-5.30pm, closed Mon-Tue; £).

Perennially popular with Hampstead folk, the Buttery Café is a delightful licensed café located at Burgh House, an 18th-century Queen Anne building that's home to Hampstead Museum (see page 84). The inside space is warm, comfortable and contemporary, while the delightful hidden garden is full of nooks and crannies. It's a civilised, tranquil retreat in which to enjoy coffee and cake or a spot of lunch with a nice glass of wine.

The café offers an array of mouth-watering, home-cooked food – both traditional British and popular European dishes – using fresh, locally sourced and seasonal produce. It's the ideal destination, whether you're seeking a delicious summer salad or a perfect winter bowl of hearty soup, or perhaps something a bit more substantial such as smoked haddock and cod fishcakes with minted pea purée or lamb and aubergine tagine with couscous. The Buttery also serves traditional afternoon tea (from 2pm), weekend brunch and a classic Sunday roast.

The reasonable prices are designed to ensure that it isn't just for a special occasion but somewhere locals can drop in when they don't want to cook, are meeting friends or just fancy a treat. It's a Hampstead institution.

Café Below

Located in the atmospheric 1,000-year-old crypt of St Mary-le-Bow church (see page 130), Café Below is one of the City's best-kept secrets. It's family-owned and run by Rachel and Anthony, whose team make all the fresh seasonal dishes in house, including bread, salad dressings, lemonade et al. The simple, reasonably-priced breakfast menu offers smashed avocado on toast, smoked salmon and scrambled eggs, and its perennial favourite bacon sandwich, while lunch includes a choice of hot mains (e.g. Korean Gochujang chicken, kimchi

style slaw and chilli roast new potatoes), salads (smoked chicken or vodka-cured salmon) and tempting puds such as treacle tart and date and apple flapjack. There's an interesting artisan wine list, a handful of cocktails and all the food is available to take away. Heavenly!

St Mary-le-Bow Church, Cheapside, EC2V 6AU (020-7329 0789; cafebelow.co.uk; Mansion House tube; Mon-Fri 7.30-10am, 11.30am-2.30pm, closed Sat-Sun; £).

Charles Dickens Museum Garden Café

This beautiful café is a serene oasis in the heart of Bloomsbury, located in an extension of the historic museum building with outdoor seating in a delightful, light-filled walled garden. The café offers a range of enticing food and drinks, including iced coffee, botanically-brewed Fentimans beverages, freshly baked cakes and savoury pastries from Paul Rhodes Bakery. For a special occasion you can hire the museum and invite up to 30 guests for a candlelit banquet in the withdrawing room. Prior to dinner, guests have exclusive access to the museum and can explore the finely-dressed historical rooms in Dickens's former home at their leisure.

Charles Dickens Museum, 48 Doughty Street, WC1N 2LX (020-7405 2127; dickensmuseum.com/pages/charles-dickens-museum-garden-cafe; Baker Street tube; Tue-Sun 10am-4.30pm, closed Mon; £).

Chez Bruce

You can be sure of a magnificent meal at Michelin-starred Chez Bruce (near Wandsworth Common), a restaurant with fine foodie credentials. In an earlier incarnation this was Harvey's, where Marco Pierre White, the enfant terrible of celebrity chefs, cut his teeth, and although more than two decades have passed since Bruce Poole and Nigel Platts-Martin took over (in 1995), it remains one of London's very best restaurants. Chez Bruce has garnered a plethora of accolades over the years, including being voted the city's favourite restaurant by gastronomes' bible *Harden's London Restaurants*.

The superb cuisine is based loosely on classical and regional French and Mediterranean cuisine. Although it may lack the histrionic flourishes and theatricality that many restaurants indulge in nowadays – and some may view this as old-fashioned – foodies delight in the wonderful cooking, relaxed ambience and superb service.

Head chef Matt Christmas is assured enough to take the odd risk and play with unusual combinations which deliver every time; the restaurant's trademarks include homemade charcuterie, slow-cooked braises, warm and cold salads, classic desserts, brilliant bread and an impeccable cheeseboard. It's all about the food at Chez Bruce and the set lunch and dinner menus are a bargain for cuisine of this quality. Naturally there's a superb wine list, including many notable and rare fine wines. It all adds up to truly refined dining.

Chez Bruce, 2 Bellevue Road, SW17 7EG (020-8672 0114; chezbruce.co.uk; Wandsworth Common rail; daily noon-2.30/3pm, 6.30-9.30/10.30pm; French/Mediterranean; ££-£££).

The Dairy

Chef Robin Gill and his wife Sarah previously worked at Le Manoir aux Quat'Saisons, so it isn't surprising that their Clapham-based bar/bistro The Dairy has received lavish praise for its superb modern British cuisine and attention to detail. The menu varies, depending on the season and on what's available in the restaurant's own urban garden (other produce is impeccably sourced), with daily specials for lunch and dinner. The four-course lunch (served Tue-Sat) is a snip at under £30, and the weekend brunch (10am-1pm) is especially popular. Don't let the unremarkable appearance of The Dairy fool you, this is seriously good cooking.

The Dairy, 15 The Pavement, SW4 0HY (020-7622 4165; the-dairy.co.uk; Clapham Common tube; Tue-Fri noon-2.30pm, 6-10pm, Sat 10am-2.30pm, 6-10pm, Sun 10am-3.30pm, closed Mon; modern British; ££).

Drawing Room Café

A handsome café secreted away in Fulham Palace alongside the Thames, the Drawing Room is a welcoming retreat occupying a pair of rather grand Georgian rooms where you can tuck into tasty food and relax on comfy sofas with free newspapers. The licensed café offers a variety of indulgent cakes and pastries, hot and cold drinks, plus a light breakfast menu during the week (full English at weekends from 9.30am to noon) and afternoon tea.

There's a seasonal lunch menu, including a choice of light hot meals, soups, sandwiches, toasties and ice-cream. And in summer the French doors open out onto a beautiful terrace overlooking the gardens, where you can enjoy barbecued food and a jug of Pimm's. Delightful!

Drawing Room Café, Fulham Palace, Bishop's Avenue, SW6 6EA (020-7736 3233; fulhampalace.org/visiting/drawing-room-cafe; Putney Bridge tube; daily 9.30am-4pm or 5pm; £).

The Gallery Café

This tranquil neighbourhood refuge is housed in a handsome Georgian building in Bethnal Green, near the Museum of Childhood. It's part of St Margaret's House Settlement, a unique charitable organisation that provides working space, support and opportunities to community organisations and charities in the London Borough of Tower Hamlets.

The café serves a tasty selection of homemade vegan food, including all-day breakfast, rolls, sandwiches, ciabattas, pizza and pasta; portions are generous and most produce is sourced locally. They also offer mouth-watering cakes, including a range of cupcakes, muffins and lemon drizzle cake, fresh juices, super coffee and a choice of teas. Housed in a light and airy space, the café provides a cosy sanctuary during the winter but is even better in summer when its suntrap terrace and gardens – with big wooden tables and parasols – come into their own.

The café hosts monthly art exhibitions, showcasing some of London's best and brightest up-and-coming talent, from illustrators and painters to mixed media artists and photography. It also takes part in the First Thursdays initiative (firstthursdays.co.uk) in which venues across East London open their doors after hours to showcase original art, culture and events on the first Thursday of the month.

Gallery Café, St Margaret's House Settlement, 21 Old Ford Road, E2 9PL (020-8980 2092; stmargaretshouse.org.uk/gallerycafe; Bethnal Green tube; Mon-Fri 8am-8pm, Sat 9am-9pm, Sun 9am-7pm; £).

The Garden Café

The Garden Café at the Garden Museum is one of London's loveliest alfresco spaces, situated on the Thames next to Lambeth Palace, almost directly opposite the Houses of Parliament. Run by award-winning chefs Harry Kaufman and George Ryle, the café is the perfect retreat from the hectic outside world, as you relax in a 17th-century-inspired knot garden while enjoying outstanding coffee and cake (baked fresh each morning) or a delicious lunch. This highly-rated oasis specialises in fresh seasonal food, including soups, salads, tarts and splendid cakes. Lunch is served from noon to 3pm, while supper is also available on Tuesday and Friday evenings.

The Garden Café, Garden Museum, 5 Lambeth Palace Road, SE1 7LB (020-7401 8865; gardenmuseum.org.uk/ page/cafe; Lambeth North tube or Waterloo tube/rail; Mon-Fri 8am-5pm, Tue/Fri 6-10pm, Sat 9am-3pm, Sun 9am-4.30pm; £-££).

The Gate Islington

This stylish, award-winning vegetarian restaurant is the younger sibling of the original Gate in Hammersmith (est. 1989), widely recognised as London's best vegan and vegetarian restaurant group (there's now a third venue in Marylebone). The food reflects the diverse cultural background of the owners, brothers Adrian and Michael Daniel, whose grandmothers blended Indian, Arabic and traditional Jewish food to create a unique culinary heritage. Ingredients are carefully sourced and inventively combined to create beautifully presented, original food combinations such as couscous-crusted aubergine, wild mushroom and celeriac rösti. The Gate offers a selection of à la carte, set menus and weekend brunch, plus a children's menu for little veggies.

The Gate, 370 St John Street, EC1V 4NN (020-7833 0401; thegaterestaurants.com/islington; Angel tube; Mon-Sat noon-10pm, Sun noon-9.30pm; vegetarian; ££).

The Harcourt

Occupying a beautiful five-storey Grade II listed Georgian building – previously home to the 19th-century Harcourt Arms pub – the handsome Harcourt is a modern Scandinavian restaurant and bar, Swedish owned and aptly located in a part of Marylebone village that's been known for over a century as Little Sweden. Spread across five rooms adorned with stunning artwork, contemporary designs and a refreshing philosophy, the Harcourt's interior, aesthetics and menu all embrace elements of Scandinavian influence and ooze *hygge* (actually Danish for cosy). Those seeking a peaceful space need look no further than the calming Garden and Summer Room, an airy glass-topped space decorated with hanging plants, lush greens and ivy-coated walls. Upstairs there are two private dining rooms offering privacy in luxurious surroundings with curated art pieces and original furnishings.

The all-day modern European menu can be enjoyed at lunch (noon-5pm) – the set lunch menu is excellent value – or dinner (6-10.30pm) and from noon on Sunday, along with an extensive wine list, while at weekends there's also a Sunday roast. Tempting starters include slow cooked organic duck egg with smoked mayonnaise, and house gravadlax; while mains feature the inevitable Nordic reindeer with smashed swede, wild mushrooms and lingonberry, and Swedish meatballs resting on a bed of homemade pasta. If you just fancy a drink there are intriguing cocktails (made with Scandinavian spirits) or you can treat yourself to Swedish afternoon tea. Skål!

The Harcourt, 32 Harcourt Street, W1H 4HX (020-3771 8660; theharcourt.com; Edgware Road tube; Mon-Sat 11am-11pm, Sun noon-10.30pm; Scandinavian; £-££).

Hereford Road

On the site of what was once a Victorian butcher's shop – as is evident from the shop window – Hereford Road is a comfortable neighbourhood restaurant offering 'simple' yet innovative British cooking. Chef Tom Pemberton, previously head chef at St John Bread and Wine, uses the best UK-sourced seasonal produce, be it meat, fish or vegetables, with impeccable provenance. Typical summer fare includes sea trout, samphire, Scottish girolles and native berries, while in winter there's mutton, game and middle white pork. The set lunch (Mon-Fri) is a steal and the wine list has been chosen with care.

Hereford Road, 3 Hereford Road, W2 4AB (020-7727 1144; herefordroad.org; Bayswater tube; Mon-Sat noon-3pm, 6-10.30pm, Sun noon-4pm, 6-10pm; British; £-££).

Honey & Co

Honey & Co. is a delightful small café-restaurant and bakery in Fitzrovia specialising in Middle Eastern cuisine. It's run by husband and wife team Itamar Srulovich and Sarit Packer, both of whom have worked at Ottolenghi (Sarit was also executive chef at Nopi) and know their *shakshouka* from their *muhamra*! It's a tiny venue with a beautiful Moroccan-tiled floor, a clutch of tables and basic white-walled décor, but don't let the small space put you off. The food here is big and bold – a treat for the eyes and the taste buds – and also good value.

Honey & Co, 25A Warren Street, W1T 5LZ (020-7388 6175; honeyandco.co.uk; Warren Street tube; Mon-Fri 8am-10.30pm, Sat 9.30am-10.30pm, closed Sun; Middle Eastern; £-££).

Leila's Shop

Owned by Leila McAlister, Leila's Shop is a bijou gem in Shoreditch, a combination of old-fashioned grocer and modern café. Farm-fresh fruit and veg are displayed outside in woven baskets, wooden crates and glazed bowls, while the rustic interior is piled high with seasonal produce and store-cupboard goodies. The peaceful café is noted for its irresistible breakfast/brunch which is served until 12.30pm − you can't go wrong with Leila's signature dish of fried eggs with sage or crisp-fried Serrano ham (served in a cast-iron frying pan) and sourdough toast. Lighter choices include homemade preserves, muesli and yoghurt, or you can just fill up on delicious coffee, croissants and cake.

Leila's Shop, 15-17 Calvert Avenue, E2 7JP (020-7729 9789; facebook.com/Leilas-Shop-251458238203777; Bethnal Green tube; Wed-Sat 10am-6pm, Sun 10am-5pm, closed Mon-Tue; £).

The Modern Pantry

With a relaxed, calm setting and charming ambience, The Modern Pantry in Clerkenwell is noted for its flavoursome, imaginative cuisine and formidable wines. Kiwi chef Anna Hansen's culinary philosophy is to excite the palate by fusing everyday dishes with unusual ingredients and global inspiration. Her food is a synthesis of

east meets west: experimental, playful and touched with magic. Not everything works perfectly, but when it does – which is most of the time – the results are sublime. There's also a separate café on the ground floor and a delicatessen next door.

The Modern Pantry, 47-48 St John's Square, EC1V 4JJ (020-7553 9210; themodernpantry.co.uk; Farringdon tube; Mon 8am-9pm, Tue-Fri 8am-10pm, Sat 9am-10pm, Sun 9am-9pm; modern fusion; ££).

Nutbourne

Situated alongside Ransome's Dock – a rare surviving Victorian anchorage just west of Battersea Park – Nutbourne is owned by the Gladwin Bros who present 'local and wild, a secret haven of Sussex countryside' on the south bank of the Thames. The menu features British seasonal produce with an emphasis on wild, foraged, locally grown and sustainable ingredients, some of which are sourced from the Gladwin family farm, such as the Sussex beef and some rather good wines. Dining is available on the spacious terrace or in the cosy spacious interior, which has a wood-fired BBQ grill.

Drop in for breakfast (Tue-Fri), lunch or dinner (Tue-Sat), or try the weekend brunch or terrific Sunday lunch. The dock is also the venue for a farmers' market on Saturdays (10am-2pm).

Nutbourne, 29 Ransome's Dock Business Centre, 27-35 Parkgate Road, SW11 4NP (020-7350 0555; nutbourne-restaurant.com; Battersea Park rail; Tue-Sat 8am-11pm, Sun 8am-5pm, closed Mon; British; £-££).

Orrery

Escape the hustle and bustle of Marylebone High Street to the sanctuary of Michelin-starred Orrery, a superb French restaurant housed in a converted stable block, boasting an elegant dining room, cosy bar and lovely rooftop terrace – one of London foodies' hidden treasures. The menus are classic French – there's even one dedicated to truffles – enhanced by inventive touches from Ukrainian chef patron Igor Tymchyshyn, complemented by an extensive, award-winning wine list. The 'lunch à la carte' menu is great value. Orrery also operates the Orrery Epicerie where you can enjoy breakfast or a light lunch and stock up on gourmet food to go.

Orrery, 55 Marylebone High Street, W1U 5RB (020-7616 8000; orrery-restaurant.co.uk; Regent's Park tube; Mon-Sat noon-2.30pm, 6.30-10/10.30pm, Sun noon-3pm, 6.30-10pm; French; ££-£££).

Pavilion Café

as rare-breed meat (from Ginger Pig), Cotswold eggs and fine Ceylon tea, to ensure that their fare stands out from the crowd.

Lunch ranges from fancy sandwiches (e.g. 'nduja and pecorino) to burgers and imaginative salads. There's also excellent coffee and tempting homemade cakes – the chocolate and marmalade is unforgettable. And you can take home freshly-baked bread, too.

Pavilion Café, Victoria Park, Crown Gate West, Old Ford Road, E9 7DE (020-8980 0030; Bethnal Green or Mile End tube; Mon-Fri 8am-4pm, Sat-Sun 8am-6pm; £).

Victoria Park – known colloquially as 'Vicky Park' – was London's first public park, opened in 1845, and is still much loved by East End folk. Its old pavilion is now home to what is widely acknowledged to be one of London's best park cafés. The Pavilion occupies a lovely domed glass building overlooking the lake, although in summer all seating is outdoors on the terrace. It's a hearty (all-day) breakfast destination, offering both workaday and classic dishes, from pancakes to full English, beans on toast and eggs every which way (Florentine, Benedict, Royale…), all served in huge portions. Owners Rob Green and Brett Redman use top-quality British ingredients, such

Petersham Nurseries Café

A destination restaurant since it opened in 2005, Petersham Nurseries is celebrated for its splendid licensed café/restaurant, where you can eat in a relaxed, convivial setting among fragrant flowers and plants at antique tables in the main glasshouse or, weather permitting, in the garden. Respecting the Slow Food philosophy (see slowfood.org.uk), which supports nutritional, sustainable and locally-produced food, the café serves seasonal Italian-inspired cuisine – its own interpretation of *aperitivo* and *cicchetti* or small plates. There's also a teahouse (open 9am-5pm, 11am Suns, no bookings).

Petersham Nurseries now has two other splendid restaurants in Covent Garden – The Petersham and La Goccia – but the original location is the most tranquil.

Petersham Nurseries Café, Petersham Nurseries, Church Lane, off Petersham Road, Richmond, TW10 7AG (020-8940 5230; petershamnurseries.com; Richmond tube; daily noon-5pm; Italian-style; ££).

Petitou

Situated off lively Bellenden Road in a 'gentrified' part of Peckham, charming Petitou occupies an old butcher's shop; the interior is all scrubbed wood, flooded with light from huge picture windows. Outside there's a hand-built ceramic terrace, scattered with tables, adorned with planters and shaded by a grand old London plane tree – the perfect spot to meet, eat and unwind. You can be assured of super coffee and cakes (the lemon polenta cake and chocolate banoffee pie are recommended) and wholesome comfort food using seasonal produce. Perennial favourites include scrambled eggs, soups, quiches, salads (served with warm flatbreads) and sandwiches on granary bread. Petitou is fully licensed and serves a selection of wines and bottled beers.

Petitou, 63 Choumert Road, SE15 4AR (020-7639 2613; petitou.co.uk; Peckham Rye rail; Mon-Sat 9am-5.30pm, Sun 10am-5.30pm; £).

Queen's Wood Café

Located in a charming late Victorian building from 1898, once home to the wood-keeper's lodge and a tearoom, this non-profit community café is tucked away among 52 acres of ancient woodland in Highgate. The owners are dedicated to the preservation and enhancement of Queen's Wood, and offer an enticing range of wholesome food and drink at affordable prices in a child- and dog-friendly environment. The café is a peaceful refuge from the hustle and bustle of the city, where you can chill and enjoy delicious organic food (with lots of vegetarian options), accompanied by a glass of beer or wine.

Queen's Wood Café, Keeper's Lodge, 42 Muswell Hill Road, N10 3JP (020-8444 2604; queenswoodcafe.co.uk; Highgate tube; May-Oct Mon-Fri 9am-5pm, Sat-Sun to 6pm, Nov-Apr Mon-Fri 10am-4pm, Sat-Sun 9am-5pm; £).

Quince Tree Café

Nestled within the grounds of Clifton Nurseries in Little Venice, a stone's throw from Regent's Canal, the Quince Tree Café occupies one of the most tranquil spots in London and is a secluded culinary gem. Its location, inside the bright and cosy palm house, makes it a perfect year-round venue. The menu includes a simple but tempting array of small lunch or sharing plates, alongside larger more substantial dishes, and there are child-friendly options, too. In addition, there's a selection of salads, nibbles, freshly squeezed juices/smoothies, some quality wines – and a brilliant breakfast/brunch menu. Enchanting!

Quince Tree Café, Clifton Nurseries, 5A Clifton Villas, W9 2PH (020-7432 1867; clifton.co.uk/the-quince-tree-cafe-london; Warwick Avenue tube; Mon-Sat 9am-5.30pm, Sun 10am-4pm; £).

The Riding House Café

Ultra-cool Riding House Café styles itself 'a modern all-day brasserie', offering breakfast, lunch, dinner, weekend brunch and Sunday lunch; there's even a separate bar with comprehensive cocktail and wine lists. You can choose from individual place settings – try the cosy, retro orange banquettes – or sit at the grand communal refectory table; there's also a secluded dining room and lounge. Food is available from 7.30am to almost midnight and includes a broad range of (fashionable) dishes, ranging from chorizo hash to chargrilled cauliflower and masala lamb chop. The menu include tapas-style small plates, full-sized brasserie mains and (on Sundays) a choice of roast – or you can just have a coffee and cake or a cocktail. You'll be spoiled for choice!

Riding House Café, 43-51 Great Titchfield Street, W1W 7PQ (020-7927 0840; ridinghouse.cafe; Oxford Circus tube; Mon-Fri 7.30am-midnight, Sat 9am-midnight, Sun 9am-6pm; British; £-££).

Rochelle Canteen

Run by an acclaimed duo of caterers, Margot Henderson and Melanie Arnold, Rochelle Canteen has long been one of London's favourite foodie spots. It's hidden behind a small door in the bike shed of the old Rochelle School in Shoreditch, and is a haven of tranquillity with a pretty garden and alfresco tables on fine days.

Open for breakfast, lunch and (Thu-Sat) supper, the outstanding cooking is all the better for its relative simplicity; the short but enticing menu changes daily and may include plaice, brown butter, capers and parsley; braised lamb shoulder, lentils, carrots and green sauce; or rabbit, potato, anchovy and rosemary. There's also a small but interesting wine list.

Rochelle Canteen, 16 Playground Gardens, E2 7FA (020-7729 5667; arnoldandhenderson.com/rochelle-canteen; Shoreditch High Street rail; daily breakfast 9am-11am, lunch noon-3pm, Thu-Sat supper 6-9pm; British; £).

The Rooftop Café

Perched on top of co-working enterprise The Exchange, in the shadow of the mighty Shard, The Rooftop Café is worth seeking out for its stunning views, spectacular roof terrace, striking décor and – especially – Peter le Faucheur's delicious food. The café serves hearty breakfasts, tasty lunches and delicious dinners (Wed-Sat). The inventive menu keeps changing but recent highlights have included squash tempura, sesame seeds, wasabi crème fraiche; crab, samphire and chilli; guinea fowl, almond quinoa, hazelnut pesto; and pistachio, lemon cake and crème fraiche. There's also an interesting wine list.

The Rooftop Café, The Exchange, 28 London Bridge Street, SE1 9SG (020-3102 3770; theexchange.so/rooftop.html; London Bridge tube/rail; Mon-Fri breakfast 8-11.45am, lunch noon-3pm, Sat breakfast 10am-1pm, brunch 1-4pm, dinner Wed-Sat 6-10pm, closed Sun; modern eclectic; £-££).

St David Coffee House

This charming, wisteria-clad café in Forest Hill is more like an eccentric aunt's front room than a coffee house, its walls lined with well-thumbed books (the café runs a book exchange) and work by local artists. The décor may be slightly kitsch but the folk who run St David are serious about their coffee, tea and delicious food, much of it homemade or sourced from local artisan producers. It's also licensed and serves craft beer. There's a large communal table by the open window for sociable sipping, or grab one of the pavement tables on a sunny day. Well worth making a trip to SE23! It's open for dinner on Fridays (6.30-11pm), too.

St David Coffee House, 5 David's Road, SE23 3EP (020-8291 6646; en-gb.facebook.com/stdavidcoffeehouse; Forest Hill rail; Tue-Fri 8am-5pm, Sat 9am-5pm, Sun 10am-4pm, closed Mon; £).

St John Smithfield

There's nowhere better to celebrate British cuisine than at the Michelin-starred St John Bar and Restaurant in Smithfield. Housed in a former Georgian smokehouse close to Smithfield Market, Fergus Henderson and Trevor Gulliver's ground-breaking restaurant is a honeypot for foodies. St John's well-sourced, traditional cuisine has stood the test of time for almost 25 years, and it remains one of the City's most reliable yet exciting places to eat. The team behind St John display an awareness of farming methods and a passion for farmers' markets and seasonal ingredients, and have long been champions of British food. There are few parts of the animal that don't find their way onto the table, from hearts to bone marrow to trotters – this is genuine nose-to-tail cooking (everything but the oink!).

The menu changes daily, but you could start with crispy pig's cheek and dandelion or roast bone marrow and parsley salad, followed by pigeon and Jerusalem artichokes or braised kid, fennel and aioli; there are fishy options, too, although this probably isn't the place to take vegetarian friends! There are also some truly splendid puds, such as twice baked chocolate cake or bread pudding and butterscotch sauce. For serious (carnivorous) foodies, there are few places to match St John.

St John Bar & Restaurant Smithfield, 26 St John Street, EC1M 4AY (020-7251 0848; stjohnrestaurant.com; Barbican tube; Mon-Fri noon-3pm, 6-11pm, Sat 6-11pm, Sun 12.30-4pm; British; ££-£££).

Wild Honey

The second restaurant from acclaimed chef Anthony Demetre (he also owns Michelin-starred Arbutus), Mayfair's Wild Honey opened in 2007 and was awarded the coveted Michelin star in its first year of trading. The bright and stylish dining space features red leather banquettes and wood-panelled walls, displaying a collection of spectacular photographs by internationally renowned photographers, while the French-inspired, daily changing menu employs fresh seasonal ingredients to produce exciting dishes. There's an interesting wine list (including organic and biodynamic wines) and superb cocktails, too. The plat du jour and working lunch/early supper menu, while not cheap, offer good value for food of this exceptional quality.

Wild Honey, 12 St George Street, W1S 2FB (020-7758 9160; wildhoneyrestaurant.co.uk; Oxford Circus tube; Mon-Sat noon-2.30pm, 6-10.30pm, closed Sun; modern European; ££-£££).

The Wren

The Wren is a non-profit coffee bar enjoying one of the City's best locations in Grade I listed St Nicholas Cole Abbey. The abbey dates back to the 12th century but was rebuilt (by Sir Christopher Wren) after the Great Fire of 1666 and again after the Second World War. Today, its soaring stone columns and beautiful stained glass windows provide a tranquil oasis in the City, and there's plenty of seating in the spacious and elegant interior plus a terrace for warmer days. In addition to seriously good coffee (Caravan) and fine tea (Brew Tea Co), there's a range of soft drinks, delicious pastries and sourdough toast, lunchtime quiches and cakes for afternoon tea. Proceeds support the work of the Abbey.

The Wren Coffee, St Nicholas Cole Abbey, 114 Queen Victoria Street, EC4V 4BJ (thewrencoffee.com; Mansion House/St Paul's tube; Mon-Fri 7am-4.30pm, closed weekends; £).

4.
Hotels & B&Bs

There are literally thousands of hotels and B&Bs in London, but it can sometimes be a challenge to find a truly quiet spot in which to lay your head. We've selected some of the capital's most tempting home-from-homes, from friendly guesthouses to luxury suites, cosy B&Bs to boutique boudoirs, traditional English period to cutting-edge contemporary. See page 4 for a price guide.

Artist Residence

A cosy boutique hotel in an elegant Regency townhouse designed by Thomas Cubitt, the award-winning Artist Residence opened in Pimlico in 2014. The welcoming façade, with smart red-and-white awnings, gives way to pared-down décor and lots of art: the hotel doubles as a gallery for a diverse range of urban, graphic and street artists. There are ten individually designed, air-conditioned rooms and suites featuring rustic, custom-made furnishings and original art, plus Smeg minibar, TV, radio and wifi. When you get the munchies, the casual-but-chic Cambridge Street Kitchen serves food all day – and you can relax in the Clarendon Cocktail Cellar or games room (complete with ping-pong table).

Artist Residence, 52 Cambridge Street, SW1V 4QQ (020-7931 8946; artistresidencelondon.co.uk; Victoria tube/rail; £-££).

Balham Lodge Guest House

This upmarket B&B – more like a small hotel really – occupies a beautiful Edwardian townhouse, situated within a conservation area adjacent to Tooting Bec Common, just 20 minutes from the West End. There's a choice of 18 tastefully-designed, comfortable en-suite bedrooms with elegant furnishings. All have tea and coffee making facilities, TV with Freeview, complimentary toiletries and wifi, while the Lodge has a 24-hour reception and off-road

parking. Breakfast – full English or continental – is served in a beautiful conservatory room with views over the patio garden and ornamental fish pond; a vegetarian option is available. If you prefer self-catering, the Lodge has two apartments (one sleeps six, the other four) a mile and a half south, overlooking Streatham Common.

Balham Lodge Guest House, 204 Bedford Hill, SW12 9HJ (020-8675 4888; balhamlodge.co.uk; Balham tube; £).

B+B Belgravia

A boutique B&B ideally located in Belgravia, occupying two Grade II listed buildings, B+B Belgravia in Ebury Street has 17 double/twin bed rooms, while nearby Studio@82 (at number 82!) offers self-catering studio apartments. The bright contemporary accommodation is complemented by an open guest lounge. A full English or continental breakfast is served in the breakfast room overlooking the garden, while studio guests receive continental breakfast delivered to their rooms. This is certainly an establishment that goes the extra mile, as facilities include free national phone calls and wifi, use of laptop and printer, free tea, coffee and mineral water, even complimentary bike hire – and it's pet-friendly, too. Note, however, that the accommodation is spread over three floors and there are no lifts!

B+B Belgravia, 64-66 Ebury Street, SW1W 9QD (020-7259 8570; bb-belgravia.com; Victoria tube/rail; £).

Charlotte Street Hotel

This elegant 5-star hotel is situated in Fitzrovia, just a few minutes' walk north from Soho Square and the theatre district. There are 52 rooms and 13 suites, all equipped with wifi, TVs and iPod docking stations, while facilities include a bar, restaurant, gym, DVD library, screening room and film club. Designer and co-owner Kit Kemp has used the 'Bloomsbury Set' as an inspiration, so the décor is a calming fusion of flowery English and avant-garde. The hotel epitomises contemporary London living – from the Oscar Bar and Restaurant that's a big hit with Bloomsbury's media crowd (try the rhubarb and lemon grass Bellini) to the luxurious private screening room – along with the all-important peaceful yet central location.

Charlotte Street Hotel, 15-17 Charlotte Street, W1T 1RJ (020-7806 2000; firmdalehotels.com/london/charlotte-street-hotel; Goodge St tube; £££).

Church Street Hotel

A cool Latin-American oasis hidden away in Camberwell, south London, Church Street Hotel is one of the capital's most unique boutique hotels. Unashamedly kitsch, the 31 rooms are each individually decorated, full of glorious bright Latin colours and throws, with funky tiled bathrooms inspired by the warmth and sensuality of the Americas. This quirky, exuberant hotel is a gem, providing attentive service, organic breakfasts and good value for money. In the Havana Lounge you can sample complimentary artisan tea and coffee or mix yourself a drink at the honesty bar, while the excellent basement Communion Bar has divine cocktails and live music. Camberwell itself is one of London's buzziest neighbourhoods with a vibrant local art scene and nightlife.

Church Street Hotel, 29-33 Camberwell Church Street, SE5 8TR (020-7703 5984; churchstreethotel.com; Denmark Hill rail; ££).

Dean Street Townhouse

Dean Street Townhouse is a luxury 5-star boutique hotel located in the centre of Soho. The handsome Grade II listed Georgian townhouse (built 1732-1735) was once home to the socially radical Gargoyle Club and the area still has a cosmopolitan vibe. There are 39 bedrooms, all individually designed and ranked by size, from tiny, cosy and small, to medium and bigger (rooms at the rear of the building on the fourth floor are the most peaceful). Each room has a king-size or super king-size bed, and TV with Sky plus, DVD, iPod dock and free wifi, while bathrooms are fitted with rainforest showers and stocked with goodies from the Cowshed spa. There's also a celebrated all-day dining room and lively bar.

Dean Street Townhouse, 69-71 Dean Street, W1D 3SE (020-7434 1775; deanstreettownhouse.com; Piccadilly Circus tube; £££).

40 Winks

An uber-chic 'micro boutique hotel' located in vibrant East London, 40 Winks occupies an elegant four-storey Queen Anne townhouse built in 1717. It's owned by David Carter (see alacarter.com), an internationally-acclaimed interior designer, whose Aladdin's cave of a home has become the B&B of choice for movie stars and fashion movers. Variously described as bold, romantic and fantastical, it's an intoxicating mix of old and new, of the seriously grand and shabby chic, exuding glamour, wit and charm. Not surprisingly, it's one of London's most popular and successful location houses, and has provided a backdrop for countless fashion and celebrity photo shoots.

The hotel grew out of requests from photographers and models to stay in the house and there are just two rooms available (one double and one single), both sharing a stunning gilded bathroom; neither has a television, although if you fancy a spot of TV there's a 'secret' television in the green 'opium den-esque' drawing room, along with a large selection of DVDs. Tea and coffee making facilities are provided, along with continental breakfast.

It really is the embodiment of a 'home from home' – like staying with an eccentric friend – where those looking for something different can enjoy a 'little bit' of understated opulence and a lavish dose of quirky style.

40 Winks, 109 Mile End Road, E1 4UJ (020-7790 0259; 40winks.org; Stepney Green tube; ££).

The Garden B&B

It would be hard to find a more peaceful retreat than The Garden B&B, located in a leafy, quiet conservation area in southwest London with direct transport links to the West End. It's an elegant Victorian house with a stunning garden, both of which have featured in magazines and on television, in Britain and overseas. There are two bedrooms – one double, one single – which are spacious, light and quiet, with TV, wifi, and tea and coffee making facilities. Aptly named, The Garden B&B's biggest asset is its award-winning garden, where you can enjoy breakfast on the terrace, indulge in afternoon tea on a summer's day or just find a quiet corner in which to chill.

The Garden B&B, Killieser Avenue, SW2 4NT (020-8671 4196; thegardenbedandbreakfast.com; Streatham Hill rail; £).

Kew Gardens B&B

An elegant and friendly B&B in a quiet street just two minutes' stroll from attractive Kew Village (and the tube into central London) and perfectly situated to explore the tranquillity of nearby Kew Gardens. There are three en-suite rooms, located on the upper floors of a glorious Victorian building

(unfortunately there's no lift!), decorated with care and flair. The owners, Scott and Ragini Annan, are vegetarian, and serve a formidable veggie breakfast in the B&B kitchen: a choice of cereals, fruit and yogurts; a selection of breads, including gluten-free; assorted porridge (including Indian) with berry compote or fruit; avocado on organic sourdough toast; and granola with berries. You can also breakfast in your room, although the choice is more limited, and then walk it all off around picturesque Kew.

Kew Gardens B&B, 8A Broomfield Road, TW9 3HR (07973-327662; kewgardensbandb.com; Kew Gardens tube; £).

The LaLiT London

Opened in 2017, The LaLiT is situated close to City Hall and Tower Bridge, and occupies an opulent, neo-Baroque red-brick building that was the former home of St Olave's Grammar School for boys (1893-1968). Inside, rich colours and contemporary furnishings proudly evoke this boutique hotel brand's Indian origins – staff wear traditional Indian dress – with flickering tea lamps, illuminated screens and gold-threaded tapestries of the tree of life. The old classrooms – some boasting 30ft (9m) high ceilings – have been transformed into 70 luxurious, Indian-themed bedrooms and suites, some offering views of the Shard or the Thames.

The hotel has two restaurants, Baluchi (in the former assembly hall) and The Terrace. Here you can explore a variety of Indian gastronomy prepared by acclaimed chefs, claimed to be 'the finest dining Indian restaurant in London'. A unique diversion is The Naan'ery where you can experience outlandishly-flavoured naan breads paired with exquisite wines. There's also a tea lounge (The Gallery), along with two bars: the Teacher's Room and the Headmaster's Room.

For the ultimate unwind, there's a luxury spa called Rejuve that offers a relaxing holistic experience combining eastern (Ayurvedic techniques) and western therapies using herbal infusions, plus the obligatory gym. It all adds up to a wonderfully calm oasis in a hectic corner of London.

The LaLiT London, 181 Tooley Street, SE1 2JR (020-3765 0000; thelalit.com/the-lalit-london; London Bridge tube/ rail; £££).

The Laslett

A contemporary boutique hotel from Tracy Lowy and Living Rooms, the delightful Laslett takes its name from Rhaune Laslett, founder of the Notting Hill Carnival. Located on a quiet street in trendy Notting Hill, the hotel comprises five elegant Victorian townhouses containing 51 delightful bedrooms and suites. Rooms feature designer

furnishings from Pinch and Race, vintage knickknacks, curated artworks, proper blankets and Neal's Yard Remedies in the bathrooms – plus Sky TV, a complimentary smartphone and Penguin Classics for bedtime reading. The hotel lobby is a popular neighbourhood hangout, incorporating a lounge, library and designer boutique, while the Henderson bar and coffee shop serves signature cocktails, brilliant breakfasts and an irresistible array of simple, seasonal dishes.

The Laslett, 8 Pembridge Gardens, W2 4DU (020-7792 6688; living-rooms.co.uk/hotel/the-laslett; Notting Hill Gate tube; ££).

My Hotel Chelsea

Opened in 2002 by Andreas Thrasyvoulou, MH Chelsea is a contemporary four-star boutique hotel in west London (there's another in Bloomsbury and one in Brighton). It features 46 bijou but elegant air-conditioned rooms and suites with great showers, free wifi, TV, DVD player, minibar and safe. Thoughtful extras include Sound Asleep pillows (available on request) into which you can plug your iPod. The heart of the hotel is The Living Room, a light and airy conservatory and bar, where you can have breakfast, plus light bites and drinks throughout the day. My Hotel offers a unique personal service and will endeavour to cater to your needs, whether it's a hypoallergenic duvet or a yoga mat. Its green credentials are noteworthy, too – there are even beehives on the roof!

My Hotel Chelsea, 35 Ixworth Place, SW3 3QX (020-7225 7500; myhotels.com/chelsea; South Kensington tube; ££).

The Penn Club

The not-for-profit Penn Club is a Quaker establishment providing B&B accommodation for members and non-members. It occupies three adjoining Georgian townhouses in Bloomsbury, retaining many original features, where previous occupants have included Jane Franklin, wife of the polar explorer Sir John Franklin, and John Wyndham, author of several sci-fi classics, including *The Day of the Triffids*, who lived and wrote at the Club during the '40s and '50s.

If you crave peace and quiet, this could be your dream home from home, as the club is blissfully calm and peaceful – almost monastically quiet. The small rooms have no TVs or radios, but free wifi is provided. Public rooms include the Edward Cadbury Room (named for the former chairman of the Cadbury Brothers confectionery company), a spacious and peaceful sitting room, a TV lounge and a dining room (where the generous breakfasts are served). Complimentary tea and coffee is available 24 hours and a small selection of snacks may be purchased, while a microwave, fridge and freezer are on hand for guests' use. Members can use the club's facilities during the day, even when not resident. Despite the fact that it's basic and quirky (no lifts), the Penn Club is extremely popular and excellent value – so book early!

The Penn Club, 21-23 Bedford Place, WC1B 5JJ (020-7636 4718, pennclub.co.uk, Russell Sq tube, £-££).

The Portobello Hotel

A charmingly eccentric hotel with an international reputation as one of London's most exclusive hideaways, The Portobello Hotel is cutting edge but with an intimate homely feel. Housed in two converted neo-classical mansions on a quiet street in Notting Hill, the 4-star Portobello has played host to famous names from the world of music, show business and fashion since it opened in 1972, but nevertheless remains a pleasingly unpretentious place, with a more civilised demeanour than its reputation might suggest.

There are 21 rooms, ranging from the cosy to the sensual, with all the usual modern conveniences such as air-conditioning, TVs and free wifi, plus some more inventive touches. Some border on the eccentric: one room has a spectacular Victorian bathing machine – a bizarre collection of copper pipes, taps and a massive sprinkler – attached to a turn-of-the-century claw-foot bath. The beds are sumptuous; some are four-posters or, in the popular Round Room, circular. Peace seekers will especially enjoy the charming basement Japanese water garden room, which has a wonderful spa bath, its own private grotto and a small garden.

In the afternoon and evening, the sitting room becomes somewhere to relax with a drink and enjoy the views over beautiful Stanley Gardens. There's a light snack menu to accompany a selection of drinks from the well-stocked honesty bar. A unique hotel with genuine warmth.

The Portobello Hotel, 22 Stanley Gardens, W11 2NG (020-7727 2777; portobellohotel.com; Notting Hill Gate tube; ££-£££).

The Rookery Hotel

With a history going back to 1784, the Rookery Hotel offers a delicious glimpse of a bygone age, with an atmosphere more redolent of a private club than a hotel, full of warmth and character, quirky but with state-of-the-art facilities. The homely interior boasts sumptuous Georgian detailing: polished wood panelling, stone-flagged floors, open fires and antique furniture. The 33 en-suite rooms are filled with more lovely old antiques, including carved oak or four-poster beds, beautiful carpets, original paintings and heavy silk curtains, while stunning bathrooms have original Victorian fittings and huge showerheads. They have modern touches, too, such as air-conditioning, TV, iPod docking, mini bar and free wifi, but a stay at the Rookery is all about the splendours of the past.

The Rookery Hotel, 12 Peter's Lane, Cowcross Street, EC1M 6DS (020-7336 0931; rookeryhotel.com; Farringdon tube; ££-£££).

The Roost

The Roost is a delightful B&B in a quiet residential area of Queen's Park, northwest London, with good transport links to the West End. The local area is alive with cafés, bars and restaurants, verdant Queen's Park and a thriving farmers' market on Sundays. The B&B occupies a large Victorian house, refurbished and decorated, with a pleasant welcoming ambience. It's filled with fine family pieces along with hostess Liz's delightful finds – an eclectic mix of furniture, objets d'art and an abundance of pictures. The three richly-dressed bedrooms are light and airy, each with a different character and style. Continental breakfast is served in a spacious Victorian conservatory overlooking a charming courtyard garden.

The Roost, 37 Lynton Road, NW6 6BE (020-7625 6770; Queen's Park tube; £).

St Pancras Renaissance Hotel

Opened in 2011, the 5-star St Pancras Renaissance Hotel occupies the lower floors of the former Midland Grand Hotel – once dubbed London's most romantic building – which was designed by Sir George Gilbert Scott and restored in the 2000s at a cost of over £150 million. Featuring 245 guest rooms, it's once again one of London's most iconic hotels, with glorious Gothic Revival metalwork, gold leaf ceilings, hand-stencilled wall designs and a grand staircase, as dazzling as the day the original Midland opened in 1873.

The communal spaces retain a sense of calm, in contrast to the frenetic activity of the station below. The old ticket hall, with soaring church-like windows, is now a bar, while the hotel's Gilbert Scott restaurant – run by celebrated chef Marcus Wareing – is a destination in its own right.

St Pancras Renaissance Hotel, Euston Road, NW1 2AR (020-7841 3540; stpancrasrenaissance.co.uk; King's Cross/ St Pancras tube/rail; £££).

San Domenico House

Occupying a pair of handsome Victorian red-brick townhouses built in 1887, San Domenico House is a luxury boutique hotel located just steps away from Sloane Square in the heart of vibrant Chelsea. Owned since 2005 by the Italian Melpignano family, San Domenico is the glossy Italian equivalent of an English country house at its most florid – all gilt and silk, urns and cherubs – offering a taste of la dolce vita in west London. Acclaimed as one of London's finest boutique hotels, it contains 15 luxurious air-conditioned rooms featuring antique furniture and plush fabrics, plus a fabulous drawing room (the perfect setting for afternoon tea), business centre, fitness room, and a peaceful roof terrace where you can enjoy cocktails and light Italian fare.

San Domenico House, 29-31 Draycott Place, SW3 2SH (020-7581 5757; sandomenicohouse.com; Sloane Square tube; £££).

Searcys Knightsbridge

Searcys Knightsbridge, aka 30 Pavilion Road, is an elegant Georgian townhouse housing a boutique B&B, a peaceful oasis conveniently located for shopping – Harrods and Harvey Nicks are close by and it's just minutes by tube from the West End. Operated by the hotel-restaurant chain Searcys, the property has a low-key, relaxed atmosphere and friendly service. There are no public areas – apart from the beautiful roof-top garden – so it's like staying with friends (only the service is better!) and ideal for those seeking an alternative to anonymous hotel chains.

The house was once a water pumping house servicing Hans Town – a suburb centred on Sloane Square and named after Sir Hans Sloane – and was recently refurbished with marble fire places and antique walnut panelling, while oil paintings adorn the walls and complement the colour palette, which is traditional yet sophisticated. The 11 en-suite rooms (seven doubles/twins, three singles and one family room) are individually designed with king-size beds and luxury touches. Most rooms are air-conditioned with free wifi, and there's 24-hour room service (drinks, light meals) and continental breakfast served in your room. The hotel has no restaurant or bar but there's a wealth of restaurants, cafés and bars on the doorstep and some will deliver to your room.

Searcys Knightsbridge, 30 Pavilion Road, SW1X 0HJ (020-7823 9212; 30pavilionroad.co.uk; Knightsbridge tube; ££-£££).

La Suite West

La Suite West is a striking boutique hotel located on a quiet street in Bayswater on the edge of Hyde Park – a soothing sanctuary close to the West End. Set in a long row of 19th-century Victorian townhouses, the hotel is a stark vision of black and white, with clean lines, sharp angles and sculptural forms; the corridor of inky-black marble floors leads to a startling long white marble reception desk. The hotel's dramatic design is echoed in the landscaped garden by the meticulously pruned plants, trees and hedges. The 80 guest rooms contain bespoke four-poster beds and marble bathrooms, while an infusion of Asian details add a touch of Zen to the hotel's minimalist design.

La Suite West, 41-51 Inverness Terrace, W2 3JN (020-7313 8484; lasuitewest.com; Bayswater tube; ££).

Temple Lodge Club

The Temple Lodge Club, a non-profit B&B, is located in an elegant Georgian building in Hammersmith, once home to the painter Sir Frank Brangwyn; his former studio on the mezzanine floor is now a celebrated vegetarian restaurant (The Gate). Sheltered from the hustle and bustle of nearby Hammersmith – guests enter a courtyard via the Angel Gate and there's also a secluded landscaped garden – it's just a few minutes from transport links yet is a serene and peaceful haven. Membership of the club – just £1 per annum – is payable with the deposit or upon arrival, and allows guests to use the facilities, which include a library and reading room.

Temple Lodge Club, 51 Queen Caroline Street, W6 9QL (020-8748 8388; templelodgeclub.com; Hammersmith tube; £).

Town Hall Hotel

The Town Hall Hotel (Grade II listed) occupies a landmark Edwardian building, dating from 1910 that was once Bethnal Green's council HQ. It was enlarged in 1937 when splendid Art Deco interiors were added, but fell into disuse in 1993. Rescued in 2007, it has been beautifully restored and converted into the luxurious 5-star hotel you see today. The award-winning building combines architectural splendour with cutting-edge design, creating a unique designer hotel that fuses the best of old and new (such as the 15m heated indoor swimming pool).

Upon entering the hotel you're immediately drawn to the beautiful domed roof of the elegant Art Deco entrance hall, the massive marble staircase and period ornamentation. Highlights include the sculpture on the frontage on Cambridge Heath Road by Henry Poole (1873-1928), the De Bathonia coat of arms representing wealthy local landowners, and stained glass windows and carvings showing scenes from the ballad of the Blind Beggar of Bethnal Green.

The 98 rooms, including 88 spectacular suites, are furnished with unique vintage furniture and are deliciously inviting, with sheepskin rugs, barista-quality coffee making facilities, luxury toiletries, an entertainment centre and free wifi. The hotel is also home to the superb Corner Room restaurant and an innovative cocktail bar offering over 200 spirits, beers and cocktails.

Town Hall Hotel, Patriot Square, Bethnal Green, E2 9NF (020-7871 0460; townhallhotel.com; Bethnal Green tube; ££).

The Ville's B&B

The Ville's is a boutique B&B situated in a quiet, residential street in the popular Villes' area of Parsons Green, just a short stroll away from the vibrant and buzzing restaurants, cafés, pubs, boutiques and antique shops of Chelsea and Fulham. The period terraced house is beautifully decorated throughout, with a calm and peaceful atmosphere. French doors lead out onto a charming roof terrace with sun loungers, table and chairs, surrounded by sweet-smelling jasmine, wisteria, passion flowers and roses, and views over London's roof tops. There are just three delightful, spacious bedrooms (two doubles – one en-suite – and one twin) equipped with LCD TV, wifi, hairdryers, bathrobes and hospitality trays. A hidden treasure.

The Ville's B&B, 39 Brookville Road, SW6 7BH (020-7381 2093; thevillesbedandbreakfast.co.uk; Parson's Green tube; £).

Zetter Townhouse

The Zetter Townhouse is a fabulous boutique hotel occupying a Georgian townhouse in Clerkenwell's St John's Square, just a few minutes from the City and West End. Lavish and luxurious, this hotel is a ravishing Aladdin's cave, bursting with character, colour and invention, a refreshing oasis in the bland world of corporate hotels. The 13 rooms range from the small but perfectly formed Club rooms, through Deluxe rooms with king-size beds, to spacious Suites – there's even an apartment if you have several cats to swing.

Those in the know come to the Zetter Townhouse for its much-vaunted cocktail lounge, run by drinks titan Tony Conigliaro. And if you're hungry, there are tasty sharing snacks, such as chicken liver parfait, Loch Duart potted salmon and hot salt beef, while the basement offers up a games room with 3D TV and table tennis.

Zetter Townhouse, 49-50 St John's Square, EC1V 4JJ (020-7324 4567; thezettertownhouse.com; Farringdon tube; ££).

5.
Libraries

Libraries, by their very design and function, are peaceful places – indeed, noisy folk are quite likely to be shown the door – so where better to seek a place for quiet contemplation? London is especially rich in libraries covering all manner of subjects, from local history to national archives, poetry to printing, politics to the performing arts. Here are some of the city's best. The libraries featured offer free public access unless stated otherwise.

Barbican Library

In spite of its bleak appearance and vast size, the 40-acre Barbican Estate is a surprisingly peaceful place. Grade II listed, this prominent example of British Brutalist architecture is also home to Europe's largest arts and conference venue. The Barbican Centre stages a comprehensive range of art, music, theatre, dance, film and creative learning events. It also has nice gardens, a glorious conservatory and one of London's best libraries.

Opened in 1982, the Barbican Library is the largest of the City's lending libraries and includes a major music library (including listening facilities and practice pianos) as well as a lively children's section. The library holds over 125,000 volumes, with special collections on London history, financial analysis, arts, classic crime and spoken word recordings. It also stocks a large collection of CDs (the largest of any UK public library), DVDs and Blu-ray disks, including the latest releases and classics, boxed sets of popular TV series and titles for children. The travel section includes a comprehensive range of maps, travel guides and language courses, and there are also reference works such as directories and telephone books available for consultation.

The library has free wifi access, 24 computer terminals, laptop points, and printing and self-service photocopying facilities. Just as importantly, there are also a number of study spaces and quiet areas where you can relax and read the wide-ranging collection of periodicals and newspapers. Other services include a regular programme of talks and events, and monthly art exhibitions in the foyer.

Barbican Library, Level 2, Barbican Centre, Silk Street, EC2Y 8DS (020-7638 0569; barbican.org.uk/visitor-information/barbican-library; Barbican tube; Mon, Wed 9.30am-5.30pm, Tue, Thu 9.30am-7.30pm, Fri 9.30am-2pm, Sat 9.30am-4pm).

Bethnal Green Library

This East London library, on the edge of Bethnal Green Garden, is housed in a handsome Victorian building dating from 1896 that was part of a notorious lunatic asylum, before becoming a place of learning in 1922. Grade II listed, the library building has many interesting historical features, including stained glass windows in memory of victims of the First World War and another portraying a famous East-End figure, the Blind Beggar of Bethnal Green. It also features cameos on the walls of important individuals such as Karl Marx, Charles Darwin and Richard Wagner. Recently restored and modernised, the library has an extensive collection of books, magazines and daily newspapers, plus free wifi, computers, scanning and printing facilities.

Bethnal Green Library, Cambridge Heath Road, E2 0HL (020-7634 6308; ideastore.co.uk/bethnal-green-library; Bethnal Green tube; Mon-Wed, Fri 10am-6pm, Thu 10am-8pm, Sat 9am-5pm).

Bishopsgate Institute Library

The Bishopsgate Institute is a celebrated cultural society established in 1895 and housed in a Grade II* listed building, described as 'a home for ideas and debate, learning and enquiry, and a place where independent thought is cherished'. The Institute's library is a free independent library that holds important historical collections and archives about London, the labour movement, free thought and cooperative movements, as well as the history of protest and campaigning, from the early 19th century to the present day. It's also stocked with newspapers, periodicals and magazines, and offers free wifi and a café.

Bishopsgate Institute Library, 230 Bishopsgate, EC2M 4QH (020-7392 9200; bishopsgate.org.uk/library; Liverpool Street tube/rail; Mon-Fri 10am-5.30pm).

British Library

The British Library (Grade I listed) is the national library of the UK, with a collection of over 150 million items covering all disciplines, from archaeology to zoology, in a wide range of formats. It's also a legal deposit library, which means that (by law) it holds a copy of every book (journal, map, etc.) published in the UK. It's free to visit the library, the exhibition galleries and tour the building, although those aged under 18 must be accompanied by an adult. The exhibition galleries include the fascinating Sir John Ritblat Gallery, which contains a permanent display of many of the library's greatest treasures, the Philatelic Exhibition containing 80,000 items and the Conservation Uncovered exhibition.

There are 11 reading rooms, each specialising in a different subject area or type of material and with different opening hours. Here you can consult books, journals and other items from the extensive collections, access a wide range of electronic resources and journals, obtain help from specialists at the reference enquiry desks, and consult subject guides, bibliographies and other research aids. Visitors need to register for a free 'reader pass' (see website) to use the reading rooms.

There's also a café and restaurant, the latter offering superb views of the six-storey King's Library, which houses 65,000 books collected by George III.

The British Library, 96 Euston Road, NW1 2DB (020-7412 7332: bl.uk; King's Cross/St Pancras tube/rail; Mon-Thu 9.30am-8pm, Fri 9.30am-6pm, Sat 9.30am-5pm, Sun 11am-5pm).

Lindisfarne Gospels

Guildhall Library

A public reference library specialising in the history of London, particularly the City of London, the Guildhall's collection comprises over 200,000 items dating from the 15th to 21st centuries, including books, pamphlets, periodicals, trade directories and poll books. The collection covers all aspects of life in London, past and present, its trades, people and buildings. The library also holds extensive collections  covering such subjects as maritime history, business history, clocks and clockmakers, wine and food, historic English law reports, and British parliamentary papers and statutes. Visitors are welcome to use the library as a study space, where a team of knowledgeable staff are on hand to assist and advise.

Guildhall Library, Aldermanbury, EC2V 7HH (020-7332 1868; cityoflondon.gov.uk/things-to-do/guildhall-library; Bank tube; Mon-Fri 9.30am-5pm, Wed 7.30pm, selected Sats 9.30am-5pm).

Kensington Central Library

Designed by Emanuel Vincent Harris in Neo-Renaissance style, the imposing Kensington Central Library opened in 1960; initially the library was far from universally popular and its design was met with demonstrations. Now Grade II* listed, this vast library houses a huge selection of books, periodicals, DVDs and CDs, and also sells ex-loan books for as little as 20p. There are large communal tables on the second floor for those wishing to study and the library also offers free wifi and the use of PCs, printers and photocopiers. There's a lovely courtyard, meeting rooms and a lecture theatre available to hire, too.

Kensington Central Library, 12 Phillimore Walk, W8 7RX (020-7361 3010; rbkc.gov.uk/libraries/libraries; Kensington High Street tube; Mon-Tue, Thu 9.30am-8pm, Wed, Fri-Sat 9.30am-5pm).

London Library

The London Library is the world's largest independent lending library, with over one million volumes in 50 languages and some 675,000 titles. Founded in 1841 by Thomas Carlyle and others, the vision was to establish an institution that would allow subscribers to enjoy the riches of a national library in their own homes. The library has occupied its current address in St James's Square since 1845, although it has been much enlarged and developed over the years, with four reading rooms and a club-like atmosphere providing a unique environment for quiet study. Membership (over 8,000) is open to all (£510 per year, £15 daily).

London Library, 14 St James's Square, SW1Y 4LG (020-7930 7705; londonlibrary.co.uk; Green Park or Piccadilly Circus tube; Mon-Wed 9.30am-8pm, Thu-Sat 9.30am-5.30pm; membership fee).

London Metropolitan Archives

Established in 1997, the London Metropolitan Archives (LMA) are home to the main archives for the Greater London area, financed by the City of London Corporation. The extensive holdings encompass over 72 miles of records of local,

regional and national importance, the earliest dating from 1067 – a year after the Norman Conquest. LMA holds a vast and diverse collection of archives, records, images, films and maps – from court reports and parish records to local government documents – relating to all aspects of London's history and charting its development into a major world city. Visitors who wish to access original material at LMA must register and obtain a History Card (details are on the website).

London Metropolitan Archives, 40 Northampton Road, EC1R 0HB (020-7332 3820; cityoflondon.gov.uk/lma; Farringdon tube; Mon-Thu 9.30am-4.45pm, Wed until 7.30pm, plus selected Sats – see website, closed Fri/Sun).

Marx Memorial Library

The Marx Memorial Library – established in memory of Karl Heinrich Marx (1818-1883), German philosopher, sociologist, economic historian, journalist and revolutionary socialist – is located in an elegant Georgian house in trendy Clerkenwell Green. It's a unique library dedicated to the advancement of knowledge and learning through books, periodicals and manuscripts relating to all aspects of Marxism, Socialism and the working class movement. Established in 1933 on the 50th anniversary of Marx's

Karl Marx

death, the library has been the intellectual home of generations of scholars. It contains an impressive number and variety of archives and collections, including all issues of the *Daily Worker* and *Morning Star* newspapers, the International Brigade Archive, the Bernal Peace Library, the Klugmann Collection and an extensive photograph library.

Marx Memorial Library, 37a Clerkenwell Green, EC1R 0DU (020-7253 1485; marx-memorial-library.org; Farringdon tube; Mon-Thu noon-4pm).

La Médiathèque

La Médiathèque is the largest French library in the UK, part of the Institut français in South Kensington, the cultural HQ for all things French in London. The Institut was founded in 1910 and occupies a handsome Art Deco building in Kensington, which is where you'll find La Médiathèque. This charming library comprises over 50,000 items and is the perfect place to read or study and make use of the free wifi, computers and print facilities. If you wish to borrow books you can become a member (from £30 a year), which also entitles you to free tickets and concessionary rates for Ciné Lumière, BFI Southbank, ICA and Riverside Studios.

La Médiathèque, Institut français, 17 Queensberry Place, SW7 2DT (020-7871 3545; institut-francais.org.uk/la-mediatheque; South Kensington tube; Tue-Fri noon-7pm, Sat noon-6pm).

National Archives

The gallery displays a wide range of treasures, including records relating to British history, family history and significant global events, as well as intriguing stories from the archive itself.

The National Archives stage a range of events, from free public talks on records of interest to training courses for archivists (see the website for information). There's also a bookshop, café and a tranquil outside area with a pond.

National Archives, Bessant Drive, Richmond, TW9 4DU (020-8876 3444; nationalarchives.gov.uk; Kew Gardens tube; Tue, Thu 9am-7pm, Wed, Fri-Sat 9am-5pm, closed Sun-Mon).

The National Archives in Kew are the official archives of the UK government (and of England and Wales) and the guardian of some of the country's most iconic national documents dating back over 1,000 years. Anyone aged 14 or over can access original documents upon producing two acceptable proofs of identity and obtaining a free reader's ticket.

The interactive museum showcases some of the diverse treasures of the archives, which range from the Magna Carta to Jane Austen's will. It stages exhibitions on selected subjects from its records and also traces the history of the National Archives and record keeping. One of the highlights is the Keeper's Gallery – the 'keeper' is the guardian and head of the archive – an exhibition space which showcases highlights from the collection.

Gold Seal of Henry VIII

Magna Carta

National Art Library

The UK's major public reference library for fine and decorative arts has a glorious location in the Victoria & Albert Museum, occupying the historic reading rooms (Grade II listed) overlooking the John Madejski Garden. The library is also the museum's curatorial department for the art, craft and design of the book; its collection numbers more than a million items, from children's books to illuminated manuscripts, and is continually growing. It's free to join – all you need is current ID with proof of address, e.g. a driving licence, passport, student card, utility bill or national identity card – and you can do so in person or online (see the website).

National Art Library, Victoria and Albert Museum, Cromwell Road, SW7 2RL (020-7942 2563; vam.ac.uk/page/n/national-art-library; South Kensington tube; Tue-Sat 10-5.30, Fri until 6.30pm, closed Sun-Mon).

National Poetry Library

Founded in 1953 by the Arts Council to promote the reading of poetry for people of all ages, cultures and backgrounds, the National Poetry Library moved to its current home at the Royal Festival Hall in 1988. It's the largest public collection of modern and contemporary verse in the world, dating from 1912 to the current day, and contains over 200,000 items. Poetry is available in many formats: books, pamphlets, audio

cassette, CD, video and DVD, for reference and loan; magazines, press cuttings, photographs, posters and postcards for reference. The library aims to stock all poetry titles published in the UK, along with a representation of work from other countries. The library is free to join – see website for details.

National Poetry Library, Level 5, Royal Festival Hall, Southbank Centre, SE1 8XX (020-7921 0943; nationalpoetrylibrary.org.uk; Waterloo tube; Tue-Sun 11am-8pm).

Pancras Square Library

A new public library run by Camden Council, Pancras Square Library is a modern, bright space with the latest fiction and non-fiction books, audio books, CDs and DVDs; a selection of large print titles, plus a wide range of newspapers and magazines. There's also a PC suite with computers and tablets, internet access (free for members) and free wifi. Other areas include a children's library, a youth zone and a jobzone, containing job-hunting materials and online research help. If you just wish to chill out and read or surf the net, there are lots of tables and a welcoming café.

Pancras Square Library, 5 Pancras Road, N1C 4AG (020-7974 4444; camden.gov.uk/libraries; King's Cross/St Pancras tube/rail; Mon-Sat 8am-8pm, Sun 11am-5pm).

RHS Lindley Library

An unusual and elegant library, the Royal Horticultural Society's collection is the largest of its kind in the world and is located at the RHS HQ in Westminster. The library's roots lie in the collection of English botanist John Lindley (1799-1865) containing many rare books dating back to 1514. More modern media includes garden guidebooks, trade catalogues, postcards and press cuttings. As well as horticulture, the collection covers

flora, birds and other related subjects. The Upper Reading Room is open to the public and holds 20th-century material available for loan, along with gardening magazines from around the world. Visitors wishing to use the Lower Reading Room, which houses the historical collections, must register.

RHS Lindley Library, 80 Vincent Square, SW1P 2PE (020-7821 3050; rhs.org.uk/education-learning/libraries-at-rhs/visit-the-libraries/lindley-library-london; Victoria rail/tube; Mon-Fri 10am-5pm).

RIBA Library

Established in 1834, the Royal Institute of British Architects (RIBA) Library is the finest architectural library in Europe, containing some four million items, including over 150,000 books, 2,000 periodical titles, one million drawings, 1½ million archive items and 1½ million photographs. Related subjects, such as construction, engineering, landscape architecture,  interior design, planning and law, are also represented in the collections. The photographing of books and periodicals is permitted for the purposes of non-commercial research and private study (photocopiers and scanners are provided). Visitors can access the library free of charge, although you're required to sign in with a photo ID or RIBA membership card.

RIBA Library, The Royal Institute of British Architects, 66 Portland Place, W1B 1AD (020-7307 3882; architecture. com/contact-and-visit/riba-library; Regent's Park tube; see website for opening times).

Royal Academy Library

Established at the time of the Royal Academy's foundation in 1768, the RA Library is the oldest institutional fine arts library in the UK. The library contains a comprehensive collection of books and exhibition catalogues on British art, artists and architects, with an emphasis on the life and practice of past and present members of the Royal Academy, and the history of the institution, its exhibitions and collections. The library also holds a special collection of illustrated books, which highlights the contribution of British artists to the illustration and design of the book. The research library and archive is open to the public by appointment.

The Royal Academy Library, Royal Academy, Burlington House, W1J 0BD (020-7300 5737; royalacademy.org.uk/ page/collections-and-research; Green Park tube).

Senate House Library

The University of London's central library houses more than two million books, 50 special collections and 1,800 archival collections on all aspects of the arts, humanities and social sciences. It's located in spectacular Senate House, an Art Deco '30s treasure that has appeared as a backdrop in numerous films, including some of the *Batman* series.

The library is at the centre of the greatest concentration of collections anywhere in the world. The research collections specialise in literature, the arts and social sciences; subject areas include art history, Commonwealth studies, English studies, film and media, Latin American studies, music, philosophy, psychology, religious studies, social sciences and Western European languages. The historic collection contains a wealth of manuscripts, archives, printed materials and maps, including primary source materials from medieval times to the modern age, and is exceptionally strong in literature and the arts, sociology, politics and economics.

Readers also have access to a wide range of eResources and databases, which is available outside of the physical Library for many membership types. Access to Senate House Library is open to members of the public (see website for fees) who can purchase a day ticket or join for three months or a year.

Senate House Library, 4th Floor, Senate House, Malet Street, WC1E 7HU (020-7862 8500; senatehouselibrary. ac.uk; Russell Square tube; opening times vary – see website; membership fee).

Swiss Cottage Library

Housed in a landmark Brutalist building (Grade II listed) designed by Sir Basil Spence and opened in 1964 – the dramatic interior is even more striking than the exterior, with mirror-image staircases and sweeping curves – Swiss Cottage Library is the largest library in the borough of Camden. Recently remodelled it has extensive seating  and study areas plus a wide range of facilities, including a large IT suite (with 50 computers), an art gallery and a café. Its collection not only includes printed books but talking books, CDs and DVDs, newspapers, periodicals, self-help leaflets, music scores, and a special historical collection of philosophy and psychology books.

Swiss Cottage Library, 88 Avenue Road, NW3 3HA (020-7974 4444; camden.gov.uk/ccm/navigation/leisure/libraries-and-online-learning-centres/swiss-cottage-library; Swiss Cottage tube; Mon-Thu 10am-8pm, Fri-Sat 10am-5pm).

Wellcome Library

The Wellcome Library (maintained by the Wellcome Trust) is based on the collection of Sir Henry Wellcome (1853–1936), who created one of the most comprehensive archives of the 20th century. Wellcome's main interest was the history of medicine, but the collection extends to subjects such as alchemy and witchcraft, plus anthropology and ethnography. You can access the library by signing in as a day visitor – which provides access to the wifi and all the material on the library shelves – or you can become a member free of charge and obtain a five-year library card. The reading room is an especially cosy place to study, with comfortable chairs and cushions, and hanging copper lamps.

Wellcome Library, 183 Euston Road, NW1 2BE (020-7611 8722; wellcomelibrary.org; Euston Square tube; Mon-Wed, Fri 10am-6pm, Thu 10am-8pm, Sat 10am-4pm).

Westminster Reference Library

Established in 1928, Westminster Reference Library is a specialist public reference library in the West End, located directly behind the National Gallery (it was built on the site of Sir Isaac Newton's house and observatory). The library specialises in art and design, business, law, performing arts and UK official publications, and its art and design collection is of national significance, containing over 40,000 volumes covering painting and drawing, fashion and furniture, architecture and antiques, ceramics and sculpture, textiles and jewellery, graphics and gardens, interiors and installations. Library facilities include computers with internet access, many online resources and three reading rooms with free wifi.

Westminster Reference Library, 35 St. Martin's Street, WC2H 7HP (020-7641 1300; westminster.gov.uk/library-opening-hours-and-contact-details; Leicester Square tube; Mon-Fri 10am-8pm, Sat 10am-5pm).

Women's Library

The origin of the Women's Library derives from the London National Society for Women's Suffrage, established in 1867, though the library wasn't formally created until the '20s. In 2013, the library was transferred from London Metropolitan University to the London School of Economics and Political Science (LSE). The collection documents all aspects of women's lives, with a particular emphasis on women in the UK and the great political, economic and social changes of the past

150 years. There's open access to the reference-only collection on the 3rd floor of the library, but if you wish to access the special collections you must order material and read it in the reading room on the 4th floor.

The Women's Library, LSE Library, 10 Portugal Street, WC2A 2HD (020-7955 7229; lse.ac.uk/library/collections/collection-highlights/the-womens-library; Temple tube; Mon-Fri 10.30am-5pm).

6.
Museums & Galleries

Most museums and galleries were designed as a backdrop to peaceful contemplation and are the perfect place to escape the madding crowds – and even if some exhibits aren't a feast for your eyes, they generally leave your ears in peace. Many offer free entry, so you can pop in for a few minutes or a few hours, rest your feet and even have a drink or meal (many have cafés). Entry is free unless stated otherwise.

Benjamin Franklin House

Benjamin Franklin

This architecturally-important (Grade I listed) house near Trafalgar Square was built around 1730 and is the only surviving home of Benjamin Franklin (1706-1790), statesman, philosopher, writer and inventor. Franklin was born in Boston, Massachusetts, but lived and worked in this house for 16 years until the eve of the American Revolution. He was a key founder of the USA and the only statesman to sign all four documents that created the new nation. As a scientist, he was a major figure in the American Enlightenment and the history of physics for his discoveries and theories regarding electricity. The inventive museum comprises several sections, including a live performance, with lighting, sound and visual projections, that brings the whole 18th-century experience to life.

Benjamin Franklin House, 36 Craven Street, WC2N 5NF (020-7839 2006; benjaminfranklinhouse.org; Charing Cross tube; tours daily except Tue, see website for details; fee).

Brunei Gallery

The Brunei Gallery at the School of Oriental and African Studies (SOAS) hosts a programme of changing contemporary and historical exhibitions, plus a permanent display of the school's remarkably rich but little known collections. The gallery was built as a result of an endowment from the Sultan of Brunei Darussalam and inaugurated by the Princess Royal in 1995. Its aim is to present and promote the cultures of Asia, Africa and the Middle East, as both a student resource and a public facility. The gallery contains exhibition spaces on three floors, a bookshop, lecture theatre, plus conference and teaching facilities – and for those needing some quiet time, there's a serene Japanese-style roof garden.

Brunei Gallery, School of Oriental and African Studies (SOAS), University of London, Thornhaugh Street, WC1H 0XG (020-7637 2388; soas.ac.uk/gallery; Russell Square tube; Tue-Sat 10.30am-5pm, Thu until 8pm).

Brunel Museum

The Brunel Museum celebrates the life and work of three generations of the legendary Brunel engineering family: Sir Marc Isambard Brunel (1769-1849), his celebrated son, Isambard Kingdom Brunel (1806-1859) – widely considered to be Britain's finest ever engineer – and Isambard's second son, Henry Marc Brunel (1842-1903), also a civil engineer.

The museum is located above the Thames Tunnel in the Brunel Engine House in Rotherhithe, designed by Sir Marc, and part of the infrastructure of the tunnel that contained steam engines to pump water from the tunnel. A permanent exhibition tells the story of the construction and history of the tunnel, including display panels, models of the tunnel under construction, original artefacts and a video presentation. On certain days (see website) you can also visit the Grand Entrance Hall above the tunnel.

Isambard Kingdom Brunel was even more famous than his father. He built dockyards and the fastest railway in the world, the 7ft broad gauge Great Western; constructed a series of steamships, including the first propeller-driven transatlantic steamship, the *SS Great Britain*; and engineered numerous important bridges and tunnels. His designs revolutionised public transport and modern engineering.

The fascinating museum also has a café, bookshop and attractive landscaped grounds, circling Brunel's original shaft and overlooking a peaceful stretch of the Thames.

Brunel Museum, Railway Avenue, SE16 4LF (020-7231 3840; brunel-museum.org.uk; Rotherhithe rail; daily 10am-5pm; fee).

Sir Marc Isambard Brunel

Isambard Kingdom Brunel

Burgh House & Hampstead Museum

Burgh House (Grade I listed) – built in 1704 in the time of Queen Anne and named after Reverend Allatson Burgh who purchased it in 1822 – is a handsome building and one of the oldest houses in Hampstead, with its original panelled rooms and staircase. It's now home to Hampstead Museum, which traces the village's long history from prehistoric times to the present day, and holds over 3,000 objects. Most exhibits relate to social history, fine art, and notable former Hampstead residents, of which there have been many. There's a display dedicated to painter John Constable, who lived in Hampstead for many years, and to poet John Keats, who lived there for a short time (see page 92). The house also hosts the superb Buttery Café (see page 34).

Burgh House & Hampstead Museum, New End Square, NW3 1LT (020-7431 0144; burghhouse.org.uk; Hampstead tube; Wed-Fri & Sun, noon-5pm, closed Mon-Tue & Sat).

Dorich House Museum

Dorich House (near Richmond Park) was the studio, gallery and home of the sculptor Dora Gordine (1895-1991) and her husband, the Hon. Richard Hare (1907-1966), a professor of Russian literature. The house is a fine example of Art Deco design, its severe exterior concealing the warmth of the splendid interior, built in 1936 and restored by Kingston University in 1994. The museum houses the world's largest collection of Gordine's bronzes and plaster sculptures, as well as many of her paintings and drawings, along with Hare's collection of Russian icons, paintings, ceramics, glassware, metalwork, folk art and furniture, dating from the 18th to 20th centuries.

Dorich House Museum, 67 Kingston Vale, Kingston-upon-Thames, SW15 3RN (020-8417 5515; dorichhousemuseum.org.uk; Kingston or Putney rail then bus 85; Thu-Sat 11am-5pm; fee).

Dulwich Picture Gallery

Designed by Sir John Soane and opened in 1817, Dulwich Picture Gallery was England's first purpose-built public art gallery. Soane's design, which made the most of natural daylight, created the prototype for modern galleries; indeed, Dulwich has been described as 'the world's most beautiful art gallery'. It's an elegant piece of abstract classicism, constructed from brick with Portland stone detailing, enclosed by peaceful gardens, mainly lawns, with a number of old and unusual trees.

The art within was mainly bequeathed by Frenchman Noël Desenfans (1745-1807) and his Swiss partner Sir Francis Bourgeois (1753-1811), who together formed one of the most successful art dealerships in Georgian London. The dealers were commissioned by Stanislaus Augustus, King of Poland, to create a Royal Collection-cum-National Gallery, but Poland was partitioned by its more powerful neighbours, leading (in 1795) to the King being forced to abdicate – and the dealers were left with a royal collection on their hands!

The collection was eventually left to Dulwich College to be put on permanent public display in a purpose-built gallery. It's a small-but-beautifully-formed gem, largely comprising well-chosen European Old Masters from the 17th and 18th centuries, including works by Canaletto, Constable, Gainsborough, Hogarth, Murillo, Rembrandt, Reynolds, Rubens and Van Dyck. There's also a superb café.

Dulwich Picture Gallery, Gallery Road, Dulwich SE21 7AD (020-8693 5254; dulwichpicturegallery.org.uk; West/North Dulwich rail; Tue-Sun 10am-5pm, closed Mon; fee).

Estorick Collection

The Estorick Collection is a hidden treasure housed in a handsome Grade II listed Georgian house in Islington. Founded in 1909, it's Britain's only gallery devoted to modern Italian art containing one of the world's best collections of early 20th-century Italian art, particularly that

of the Futurism movement. As well as paintings, the collection includes sculpture and figurative art, displayed in six galleries. The collection's title comes from Eric Estorick (1913-1993), an American sociologist, writer and art collector, who became a full-time art dealer and established a foundation to which he left his Italian collection; 39A Canonbury Square, the former home and office of architect Sir Basil Spence, was purchased to house the collection. There's also an art library, bookshop and a lovely garden café.

Estorick Collection, 39A Canonbury Square, N1 2AN (020-7704 9522; estorickcollection.com; Highbury & Islington tube/rail; Wed-Sat 11am-6pm, Sun noon-5pm, closed Mon-Tue; fee).

Fan Museum

The Fan Museum opened in Greenwich in 1991 and is the only museum in the world devoted entirely to fans and fan-making. It's housed in a pair of handsome Grade II* listed early Georgian houses built in 1721, which have been lovingly restored to reveal their original character and elegance. An orangery, faithful to the architecture of the period, has been added, with a spectacular mural, overlooking a Japanese-style garden with a fan-shaped parterre, pond and stream – an oasis of tranquillity. The museum's collection numbers more than 4,000 fans, fan leaves and related ephemera, with the oldest dating from the 11th century – the stars are the rare and beautiful 18th- and 19th-century European fans. Afternoon tea is served in the tranquil orangery on Tue and Fri-Sun (12.30-4.30pm).

Fan Museum, 12 Crooms Hill, SE10 8ER (020-8305 1441; thefanmuseum.org.uk; Cutty Sark DLR; Tue-Sat 11am-5pm, Sun noon-5pm, closed Mon; fee).

Fenton House

Named after the Fenton family who purchased it in 1793, Fenton House is a charming 17th-century merchant's house built around 1686, which has been virtually unaltered during 300 years of continuous occupation. Now owned by the National Trust, the house is home to a collection of early keyboard instruments compiled by the many-named Major George Henry Benton Fletcher (1866-1944), and also boasts important collections of paintings (by the likes of Jan Bruegel, Albrecht Dürer, John Russell, Francis Sartorius and GF Watts), porcelain, 17th-century needlework pictures and Georgian furniture. The enchanting garden, laid out on the side of a hill, is a rural haven.

Fenton House, Hampstead Grove, NW3 6SP (020-7435 3471; nationaltrust.org.uk/fenton-house-and-garden; Hampstead tube; March to October/November, Wed-Sun 11am-5pm, closed Mon-Tue; fee).

Florence Nightingale Museum

The Florence Nightingale Museum tells the engrossing story of one of Britain's greatest heroines. From the slate she used as a child to the Turkish lantern she carried in the Crimean War – which earned her the sobriquet 'The Lady with the Lamp' – the collection spans the life of Florence Nightingale (1820-1910) and her nursing legacy. She's most famous for taking a team of nurses to the Crimea to care for thousands of wounded soldiers during the Crimean War, which saved the British army from medical disaster. Florence was a visionary health reformer, a brilliant campaigner and the second most influential woman in Victorian Britain after Queen Victoria.

Florence Nightingale Museum, St Thomas' Hospital, 2 Lambeth Palace Road, SE1 7EW (020-7188 4400; florence-nightingale.co.uk; Lambeth North or Westminster tube; daily 10am-5pm; fee).

Florence Nightingale

Foundling Museum

One of London's most intriguing collections, the Foundling Museum is located in a leafy cul-de-sac in Bloomsbury. It tells the story of the Foundling Hospital, London's first home for abandoned children, which involves three major figures in British history: philanthropist Sir Thomas Coram (1668-1751), artist William Hogarth (1697-1764) and composer George Frederic Handel (1685-1759). Coram founded the hospital after being appalled by the number of abandoned, homeless children living on London's streets, while Hogarth and Handel were major benefactors. The museum's collection charts the history of the hospital from its foundation in 1739 to its closure in 1954. It's a fascinating blend of art, period interiors and social history, housed in a restored building adjacent to the hospital's original home, demolished in 1928.

The museum has two principal collections. The Foundling Collection relates to the hospital itself and the stories of the 27,000 children who passed through its doors during its 215-year history. Especially poignant is the collection of tokens mothers left with their babies – coins, buttons, bits of jewellery – allowing the hospital to match a mother with her child should she ever come back to claim it, though sadly this didn't happen very often. It also includes the Gerald Coke Handel Collection, the largest privately-held collection of Handel material. The museum – which was Britain's first public art gallery – also exhibits paintings and sculptures by Hogarth, Thomas Gainsborough, Joshua Reynolds and others. There's a charming café, too.

Foundling Museum, 40 Brunswick Square, WC1N 1AZ (020-7841 3600; foundlingmuseum.org.uk; Russell Square tube; Tue-Sat 10am-5pm, Sun 11am-5pm, closed Mon; fee).

Freud Museum

An interesting, atmospheric museum is housed in the former home of Sigmund Freud (1856-1939) who fled to Britain with his family after the Nazi annexation of Austria in 1938. Built in 1920 in Queen Anne style, the handsome red-brick house remained the Freud family home until 1982, when Anna Freud, Sigmund's youngest daughter, died. Sadly Sigmund Freud died a year after arriving in London and just a few weeks after the Second World War broke out in September 1939. The museum's centrepiece is Freud's study, preserved and furnished exactly as it had been in Vienna, using Freud's notes so that it could be faithfully recreated. The house is also a showcase for Freud's impressive collection of antiquities (Egyptian, Greek, Roman and Oriental), totalling some 2,000 items. There's a beautiful garden and interesting shop, too.

Freud Museum, 20 Maresfield Gardens, NW3 5SX (020-7435 2002; freud.org.uk; Finchley Road tube; Mon, Wed-Sun noon-5pm, closed Tue; fee).

Grant Museum of Zoology

In an increasingly slick, hi-tech world, the Grant Museum has a healthy air of the Victorian collector; it's how museums used to be, with the emphasis on exhibits in cases rather than interactive displays, soundscapes and other such innovations. The Grant is London's only university zoological museum, with some 68,000 specimens covering the entire animal kingdom, including those now extinct such as the dodo and quagga; it's also home to around one million insects, the most abundant group of creatures in the world. It was named after Robert Grant (1793-1874), the first Professor of Zoology and Comparative Anatomy in England, and was founded in 1828 as a teaching collection; this remains the basis of the museum, along with exhibits donated by Thomas Henry Huxley.

Grant Museum of Zoology, Rockefeller Building, 21 University Street, WC1E 6DE (020-3108 2052; ucl.ac.uk/culture/grant-museum-zoology; Euston Square tube; Mon-Sat, 1-5pm, closed Sun).

Guildhall Art Gallery

The Grade I listed Guildhall was built between 1411 and 1440 and is a rare and magnificent medieval Grade I listed landmark, the only surviving stone building in the City that doesn't belong to the Church. The Guildhall Art Gallery houses the art collection of the City of London Corporation and occupies a building designed by Richard Gilbert Scott and completed in 1999 to replace an earlier building destroyed in the Blitz in 1941. It's a beautiful stone building in a semi-Gothic style, sympathetic to the historic Guildhall, to which it's connected internally. During its construction the remains of a Roman amphitheatre were discovered beneath Guildhall Yard, which can be seen below the gallery.

The gallery was established in 1886 as 'a collection of art treasures worthy of the capital city' and shows a changing display of around 250 works from the City's collection of some 4,000 paintings, drawings and sculptures, in addition to a programme of temporary exhibitions. The collection has been accumulated by the City of London since the 17th century and includes works by Constable, Dante Gabriel Rossetti, Landseer and Millais. A rich variety of Victorian paintings can be seen as you enter the gallery, displayed in the original 19th-century style, illustrating the key artistic movements and influences of the Victorian period, from the Pre-Raphaelite Brotherhood, to Orientalism, Classicism and narrative painting.

Guildhall Art Gallery, Guildhall Yard (off Gresham Street), EC2V 5AE (020-7606 3030; guildhall.cityoflondon.gov.uk/art-gallery; Bank tube; Mon-Sat 10am-5pm, Sun noon-4pm).

Handel & Hendrix in London

Handel & Hendrix in London comprises two residences: Handel's house at 25 Brook Street and Hendrix's flat on the top floor of 23 Brook Street. Number 25 is a restored Georgian building (Grade I listed) which was home to the noted baroque composer George Frederic Handel (1685-1759) from 1723 until his death. It's where he composed some of his best works, including *Messiah*, *Zadok the Priest* and *Music for the Royal Fireworks*. The house celebrates the composer and his work with concerts, special events and exhibitions, all designed to bring Handel's world to life. The museum also aims to promote the musical and cultural heritage of 23 Brook Street, where rock legend Jimi Hendrix (1942-1970) rented a flat in 1968 with his then girlfriend, Kathy Etchingham; it's the musician's only surviving home.

Handel & Hendrix in London, 25 Brook Street, W1K 4HB (020-7495 1685; handelhendrix.org; Bond Street tube; Mon-Sat 11am-6pm, closed Sun; fee).

Horniman Museum

Opened in 1901, the Horniman Museum in southeast London is housed in a lovely Arts and Crafts and Art Nouveau-style building designed by Charles Harrison Townsend. The museum was founded by the Victorian tea trader Frederick John Horniman (1835-1906) to house his superb collection of cultural artefacts, ethnography, natural history and musical instruments, some collected personally on his travels, but mostly sourced by his tea merchants. The collection of over 350,000 objects is neither dusty nor static, and is constantly being enlarged, researched and brought into public view. The museum also has one of London's oldest aquariums, dating from 1903, plus a modern aquarium in the basement. There's also a superb café and the bonus of 16 acres of award-winning, beautifully maintained gardens, featuring a conservatory, a nature trail and a butterfly house.

Horniman Museum & Gardens, 100 London Road, SE23 3PQ (020-8699 1872; horniman.ac.uk; Forest Hill rail; daily 10am-5.30pm; fee to visit the new aquarium and butterfly house).

Institute of Contemporary Arts

One of London's leading artistic and cultural centres, the ICA contains galleries, a theatre, two cinemas, a superb bookshop and a popular bar. It's located within Nash House, part of Carlton House Terrace, a grand Regency period building on The Mall. The ICA was founded by a group of radical artists in 1946 to challenge the foundations of contemporary art, and in its early years organised exhibitions by Pablo Picasso and Jackson Pollock, and also launched Pop art, Op art, and British Brutalist art and architecture. The ICA is never afraid of breaking the rules and doing something different, so expect the unexpected – no one who's serious about contemporary art can afford to ignore it.

Institute of Contemporary Arts, The Mall, SW1Y 5AH (020-7930 3647; ica.art; Charing Cross tube/rail; Tue-Sun 11am-11pm, Fri-Sat midnight, closed Mon).

Keats House

Built 1814-1816 and Grade I listed, Keats House is the former home of John Keats (1795-1821), one of the leading poets of the English Romantic movement. Keats lodged here with his friend Charles Brown from December 1818 to September 1820, only a short period of time but one of his most productive. Soon after, he travelled to Italy where he died of tuberculosis the following year, aged just 25. The house is now a shrine to the poet and contains a huge range of Keats-related material, including books, paintings and the engagement ring he gave to Fanny Brawne (the girl next door). The garden – where Keats is said to have written *Ode to a Nightingale* – has been described as one of the most romantic in London, with plants reflecting its Regency heritage.

Keats House, 10 Keats Grove, NW3 2RR (020-7332 3868; cityoflondon.gov.uk/things-to-do/keats-house; Hampstead tube; Wed-Sun 11am-5pm, closed Mon-Tue; fee).

Leighton House Museum

Situated in Holland Park, Leighton House is the former home of painter and sculptor Lord Frederic Leighton (1830-1896). It's one of the 19th-century's most remarkable buildings – from the outside it's elegant rather than striking, but has one of London's most original interiors. Leighton was associated with the Pre-Raphaelite Brotherhood, his work depicting biblical, classical and historical subjects (his best known work is *Flaming June*), and his home is as flamboyant and colourful as its former owner.

The original house was designed in 1864 by George Aitchison and resembles an Italianate villa, constructed of red Suffolk brick with Caen Stone dressings in a restrained classical style. The building was extended over the next 30 years by Aitchison to create a private art palace for Leighton, and its centrepiece is the remarkable two-storey Arab Hall, designed to display Leighton's priceless collection of over 1,000 Islamic tiles, dating from the 13th-17th centuries and collected during his trips to the Middle East. The interior of this pseudo-Islamic court gives a stunning impression of the Orient – with gilded ceilings, peacock blue tiles, red walls and intricate black woodwork – including a dome and a fountain. Breathtaking!

Leighton House Museum, 12 Holland Park Road, W14 8LZ (020-7602 3316; rbkc.gov.uk/subsites/museums/leightonhousemuseum1.aspx; High Street Kensington tube; Mon, Wed-Sun 10am-5.30pm, closed Tue; fee).

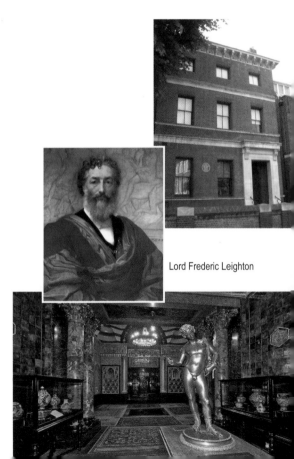

Lord Frederic Leighton

Museum of the Order of St John

The Museum of the Order of St John tells the unique and fascinating story of the Order of the Hospital of St John of Jerusalem – founded after the first Crusade captured Jerusalem in 1099 – and its more recent incarnation as St John Ambulance, established in 1877. The story spans over 900 years; beginning with the Crusades and continuing through revolutions, war and peace, it shows how warrior monks set out from Clerkenwell to fight for the faith and tend the sick. The Order originally consisted of a group of Knights who took vows of poverty, chastity and obedience and dedicated themselves to the care of the sick, but later assumed a military role and took control of Crusader castles.

The museum occupies two sites in Clerkenwell: St John's Gate (dating from 1504), the entrance to the former Priory of the Knights of St John, and the Priory Church of St John, Clerkenwell, with its surviving 12th-century crypt. The diverse collection includes rare illuminated manuscripts (such as the Rhodes Missal of 1504), armour, weapons, paintings, coins, furnishings, ceramics, silverware and textiles, plus historic first-aid equipment and St John Ambulance memorabilia. The cloister garden is an especially tranquil spot.

Museum of the Order of St John, St John's Gate, 26 St John's Lane, EC1M 4DA (020-7324 4005; museumstjohn. org.uk; Farringdon tube; Mon-Sat 10am-5pm, closed Sun).

Orleans House Gallery

One of Greater London's finest small galleries, the Orleans House Gallery is located in woodland overlooking the Thames. The house was built in 1710 and is named after Louis Philippe, Duke of Orleans and later King of France, who lived there between 1813 and 1815. Opened in 1972, the gallery displays the art collection of the borough of Richmond-upon-Thames, one of the most outstanding fine art collections in London. It comprises some 3,200 paintings, drawings, photographs, prints and objects dating from the early 18th century to the present day. The nearby Stables Gallery, housed in the 19th-century stable buildings, exhibits work by local artists. There's also a café and lovely secluded gardens.

Orleans House Gallery, Riverside, Twickenham, TW1 3DJ (020-8831 6000; orleanshousegallery.org; Twickenham rail; Tue-Sun 10am-5pm, closed Mon).

Petrie Museum of Egyptian Archaeology

Long overshadowed by the British Museum's tourist-thronged Egyptian galleries, the Petrie Museum – named after the noted archaeologist William Flinders Petrie (1853-1942), whose collection was purchased by University College London in 1913 – is an unsung wonder. Boasting around 80,000 objects, it's one of the world's great collections of Egyptian (and Sudanese) archaeology,

covering life in the Nile Valley from prehistory through the time of the pharaohs and on through the Ptolemaic, Roman, Coptic and Islamic periods. The museum provides a vivid picture of daily life through Egypt's many eras and cultures. The collection contains a wealth of personal objects – including combs, hair curlers, mirrors and razors – which reveal how ordinary Egyptians lived.

Petrie Museum of Egyptian Archaeology, University College London, Malet Place, WC1E 6BT (020-7679 2884; ucl.ac.uk/culture/petrie-museum; Euston Square tube; Tue-Sat 1-5pm, closed Mon, Sun).

Photographers' Gallery

The Photographers' Gallery in Soho was the first public gallery in the UK devoted solely to photography, offering inspiration for everyone from phone snappers to professionals. From the latest emerging talent to historical archives and established artists, it's *the* place to see photography in all its forms. Established in 1971, the gallery features three dedicated floors of gallery space, at the heart of which is the studio floor, which hosts a range of talks, events, workshops and courses, as well as a study room, a camera obscura (offering a 360 degree vertical 'slice' of the street outside) and Touchstone, a changing display of a single photographic work. Complementing the exhibition and education floors are a bookshop, a print sales gallery and a café-bar, all at street level.

Photographers' Gallery, 16-18 Ramillies Street, W1F 7LW (020-7087 9300; thephotographersgallery.org.uk; Oxford Circus tube; Mon-Sat 10am-6pm, Thu 8pm, Sun 11am-6pm).

Ranger's House & Wernher Collection

This red brick Georgian villa, built in the Palladian style, dates from the early 1700s and houses one of London's most elegant art collections. It's adjacent to Greenwich Park and became the official residence of the park's ranger in 1816 – hence the name. Since 2002 the Ranger's House has been home to the Wernher Collection – jewellery, paintings, porcelain, silver and much more – accumulated in the late 19th and early 20th centuries by Sir Julius Wernher (1850-1912). It comprises almost 700 works of art, spread over 12 rooms, including early religious paintings, Dutch Old Masters, tiny Gothic ivories, fine Renaissance bronzes, silver treasures and some of Europe's most spectacular jewellery.

Ranger's House & Wernher Collection, Chesterfield Walk, Blackheath, SE10 8QX (0370-333 1181; english-heritage. org.uk/visit/places/rangers-house-the-wernher-collection; Cutty Sark DLR or Blackheath rail; see website for opening times; fee).

Serpentine Galleries

The Serpentine Galleries comprise not one but two galleries five minutes' walk from each other on either side of the Serpentine Bridge in the heart of Kensington Gardens. The Serpentine Gallery, established in 1970, occupies a classical 1934 tea pavilion, while the Serpentine Sackler Gallery, opened in 2013, is housed in a former gunpowder store. Together they present world-renowned exhibitions of art, architecture and design, and comprise one of London's most important showcases for contemporary art.

Serpentine Gallery Pavilion

The Serpentine Gallery also hosts the Serpentine Gallery Pavilion commission, an annual programme of temporary structures by internationally acclaimed architects and designers. First presented in 2000, the series is unique and showcases the work of an international architect (or design team) who hasn't completed a building in England at the time of the gallery's invitation.

The pavilion is sited on the gallery's lawn for three months and in recent years has featured designs by Rem Koolhaas, Peter Zumthor and, in 2012, the Chinese artist-activist Ai Weiwei.

The Serpentine Sackler Gallery – named after benefactors Dr Mortimer and Theresa Sackler – occupies The Magazine (Grade II* listed and dating from 1805) with a stunning modern extension designed by award-winning architect Zaha Hadid (1950-2016). Opened in 2013, the gallery on West Carriage Drive provides more space for art and social events, as well as a permanent restaurant (Chucs Serpentine, Tue-Sun 9am-6.30pm). The Serpentine conceives and presents its programmes across both the Serpentine Gallery and the Serpentine Sackler Gallery in four seasons per year.

Serpentine Galleries, Kensington Gardens, W2 3XA/W2 2AR (020-7402 6075; serpentinegalleries.org; Lancaster Gate tube; Tue-Sun 10am-6pm, closed Mon).

Serpentine Gallery

Sackler Gallery

South London Gallery

The South London Gallery is a publicly-funded gallery of contemporary art in Camberwell. Founded in 1891, it occupied various locations until moving to its current, purpose-built home constructed of Portland stone and hand-made pressed bricks, much favoured by the Arts and Crafts tradition at the time. Internationally acclaimed artists who have staged exhibitions here include Gilbert and George, Anselm Kiefer and Sherrie Levine, as well as Gavin Turk, Ann Sofi-Sidén and Tracey Emin. Today, the SLG has an international reputation for its programme of contemporary art exhibitions and live arts events. The gallery is also home to the lovely Habit Café and has two relaxing urban gardens.

South London Gallery, 65-67 Peckham Road, SE5 8UH (020-7703 6120; southlondongallery.org; Peckham Rye rail; Tue-Fri 11am-6pm, 9pm Wed, Sat-Sun 10am-6pm, closed Mon).

Tate Britain

Venice, The Bridge of Sighs (JMW Turner)

The original Tate gallery opened in 1897 to provide a dedicated home for British art, and nowadays attracts almost two million art lovers annually. A major rebranding in 2000 saw its modern art moved down the River Thames to Tate Modern at Bankside, while Tate Britain (as it's now known) majors in historic and contemporary art – and is now a much calmer place to visit. The gallery's permanent collection dates from 1500 to the present day, and is one of the most comprehensive of its kind in the world, including works by Turner, Gainsborough, Hogarth, Constable, Stubbs, Bacon, Moore, Hockney and many others. Take time out to visit the Rex Whistler Restaurant and see Whistler's massive mural, *The Expedition in Pursuit of Rare Meats*.

Tate Britain, Millbank, SW1P 4RG (020-7887 8888; tate.org. uk; Pimlico/Vauxhall tube; daily 10am-6pm).

Victoria Miro Gallery

Victoria Miro – one of the grandes dames of the Britart scene – opened a contemporary art gallery in Mayfair in 1985, earning widespread acclaim for showcasing the work of established and emerging artists from Europe, Asia and the US, and nurturing the careers of young British artists. In 2000, the gallery moved to its present home, a former furniture factory situated between two of London's trendiest areas, Islington and Hoxton, and it now has 19,000ft² (1785m²) of artfully-lit exhibition space. The Victoria Miro Gallery is almost unique in

London (among private galleries) for having its own garden, a pretty landscaped area overlooking a stretch of the Regent's Canal, which has been used to great effect for installations by artists such as Yayoi Kusama (Japan) and Alex Hartley.

Victoria Miro Gallery, 16 Wharf Road, N1 7RW (020-7336 8109; victoria-miro.com; Angel/Old Street tube; Tue-Sat 10am-6pm, closed Mon, Sun).

Wallace Collection

Established in 1900, the Wallace Collection is one of London's best art collections and is housed in an imposing Georgian mansion dating from 1776. It's primarily the collection of the first four Marquesses of Hertford, which was bequeathed to the nation in 1897 by the widow of Sir Richard Wallace (1818-1890). It comprises many outstanding examples of fine and decorative arts dating from the 15th-19th centuries, spread over 25 galleries, including French 18th-century paintings and furniture, Sèvres porcelain, arms and armour, and Old Master paintings. The latter includes works by Canaletto, Delacroix, Fragonard, Gainsborough, Hals, Landseer, Murillo, Rembrandt, Reynolds, Rubens, Titian, Turner, Van Dyck and Velásquez. The museum has a restaurant located in a tranquil glass-roofed courtyard.

Wallace Collection, Hertford House, Manchester Square, W1U 3BN (020-7563 9500; wallacecollection.org; Bond Street tube; daily 10am-5pm).

Whitechapel Gallery

Located in a striking building with a distinctive façade designed by Charles Harrison Townsend, the Whitechapel Gallery (founded in 1901) in East London is one of Britain's most forward-thinking and influential art galleries. Noted for its excellent contemporary art exhibitions, it

famously exhibited Picasso's *Guernica* in 1938 as part of a touring exhibition and was later a pioneer of the Pop Art movement. The gallery has premiered international artists such as Frida Kahlo, Jackson Pollock and Mark Rothko, and showcased British artists, including Lucian Freud, Gilbert and George, and David Hockney. There's also a bookshop and the Whitechapel Refectory, a popular café-wine bar.

Whitechapel Gallery, 77-82 Whitechapel High Street, E1 7QX (020-7522 7888; whitechapelgallery.org; Aldgate East tube; Tue- Sun 11am-6pm, Thu 9pm, closed Mon).

William Morris Gallery

This is the only public gallery devoted to William Morris (1834-1896) – artist, designer, writer, socialist, conservationist and father of the Arts and Crafts movement – located in a substantial (Grade II* listed) Georgian building that was the Morris family home from 1848 to 1856. The house and its grounds were donated to the people of Walthamstow by the family of Edward Lloyd (1815-1890), who purchased it from the Morris family in 1856. The gallery contains a diverse collection, including printed, woven and embroidered fabrics, rugs, carpets, wallpapers, furniture, stained glass and painted tiles, designed by Morris and his artist colleagues, including Dante Gabriel Rossetti, Edward Burne-Jones and William De Morgan. There's a charming tearoom and a tempting shop, too.

William Morris Gallery, Lloyd Park, Forest Road, E17 4PP (020-8496 4390; wmgallery.org.uk; Walthamstow Central tube; Tue-Sun 10am-5pm, closed Mon).

7.
Parks & Gardens

London has a wealth of green spaces, from majestic royal parks to glorious quintessential English gardens and tranquil cemetery parks, historic horticultural gems and hidden sanctuaries to Zen-like retreats. They offer a welcome refuge from the hustle and bustle of London life and could have been designed especially with peace and quiet in mind. Many also contain welcoming cafés and are the perfect spot for an idyllic picnic. All the parks and gardens featured offer free entry.

Abney Park Cemetery

Now a memorial park and woodland nature reserve, Abney Park was originally one of London's 'Magnificent Seven' cemeteries, built by the Victorians to cope with the rapid population increase. It was laid out in the early 18th century on the instructions of Lady Mary Abney and others, becoming a non-denominational garden cemetery in 1840, and also a semi-public arboretum and educational institute. Today, Abney Park is a romantic wilderness, every bit as atmospheric and interesting as its more celebrated 'neighbour', Highgate Cemetery. Its crumbling state adds to its charm, with some magnificent urns, inscriptions, ivy-clad statues and sculptures – leaning, tumbling, falling over and merging with the planting. Abney Park is just off busy Stoke Newington High Street but the shady walks, quiet picnic spots and richness of wildlife make it feel miles away.

Abney Park Cemetery, Stoke Newington High Street, N16 0LH (020-7275 7557; abneypark.org; Stoke Newington rail; daily 8am-dusk).

Brockwell Park

One of south London's best and most diverse public parks, Brockwell Park covers 125 acres, with the late Georgian Brockwell Hall (Grade II* listed) at its heart. Opened in 1892, the park incorporates a wide range of facilities and green areas, including ornamental ponds, wetlands, a wild meadow, open grassland, community greenhouses, formal flower beds, a tranquil walled rose garden and a charming 19th-century clock tower. Sports facilities include tennis courts, a bowling green, a purpose-built BMX track, basketball, soccer, cricket, tennis courts and the magnificent Brockwell Lido, opened in July 1937 and now restored to its former glory (with a gym). The park also has a children's play area, a paddling pool and miniature railway, plus a café in Brockwell Hall.

Brockwell Park, Norwood Road, SE24 9BJ (020-7926 9000; lambeth.gov.uk/places/brockwell-park, brockwelllido.com; Brixton tube then bus 3; daily 7.30am-dusk).

Brompton Cemetery

Opened in 1840, Brompton Cemetery was the sixth of London's 'Magnificent Seven' cemeteries, extending to 39 acres in west London. It was designed by Benjamin Baud, and the grounds were laid out by landscape gardener Isaac Finnemore. Baud envisaged the cemetery as an open-air cathedral, with a tree-lined Central Avenue as its nave; the domed chapel, in honey-coloured Bath stone, as its high altar; and two long colonnades embracing the Great Circle (reputedly inspired by the piazza of St Peter's in Rome).

Now Grade I listed, Brompton is one of Britain's most distinguished garden cemeteries, containing some 35,000 monuments (many listed) and over 200,000 burial sites. It's the only Crown Cemetery still used for burials, although nowadays it's more popular as a public park than a place to remember the dead. People from all walks of life are buried here, including no fewer than 13 Victoria Cross holders. Among its most famous 'residents' is author Beatrix Potter – who lived in The Boltons nearby – who took the names of many of her animal characters from tombstones in the cemetery (such as Jeremiah Fisher and Mr Nutkins).

Lime trees predominate along the northwest and southeast avenues, with scattered mature weeping silver lime, holly, holm oak, cedar of Lebanon and yew. As well as its many attractions, the cemetery provides an oasis in all seasons and is a rare haven of peace, beauty and tranquillity in a part of London with few other green spaces.

Brompton Cemetery, Fulham Road, SW10 9UG (020-7352 1201; royalparks.org.uk/parks/brompton-cemetery, brompton-cemetery.org.uk; West Brompton tube; 7am-dusk).

Bunhill Fields

Bunhill Fields (3.7 acres) is a verdant burial ground in Islington, providing a semi-rural respite from the bustling streets surrounding it. It was never consecrated and was used for centuries to bury non-conformists and dissenters, who

weren't acceptable to the established church, and to bury plague victims in 1665. In use until 1854, by which time it was full to overflowing, Bunhill was converted into a public garden in 1868, with new walls, paths and trees. Many of the old monuments remain, the earliest still visible dating from 1666. Of particular note are monuments to John Bunyan, author of *The Pilgrim's Progress*, and Dr Isaac Watts, whose hymns are popular worldwide. Other notable interments include William Blake, Daniel Defoe and Eleanor Coade (the inventor of Coade stone).

Bunhill Fields, 38 City Road, EC1Y 2BG (020-7374 4127; cityoflondon.gov.uk/things-to-do/green-spaces/city-gardens; Old Street tube; Mon-Fri 8am-7pm or dusk, Sat-Sun 9.30am-7pm or dusk).

Camley Street Natural Park

A quiet green haven in the most urban of locations, Camley Street Natural Park is tucked away behind St Pancras International Station. Comprising a narrow strip of land (2 acres) bounded by the Regent's Canal (alongside St Pancras Lock), Camley Street is an urban wildlife sanctuary and education centre managed by the London Wildlife Trust. Open since 1985, the park is an example of the success and importance of urban ecology for environmental and educational purposes in the heart of London. A variety of habitats co-exist here, including wetlands, marshland, a wildflower meadow, woodland, reed beds around a pond and a garden area, all of which attract a plethora of insects, amphibians, birds, mammals and a rich variety of plant life.

Camley Street Natural Park, 12 Camley Street, NW1 4PW (020-3897 6150; wildlondon.org.uk/reserves/camley-street-natural-park; King's Cross/St Pancras tube/rail; Mon-Fri, Sun 10am-4pm, closed Sat).

Cannizaro Park

park has a large variety of green spaces, from expansive lawns and leisurely walks through woodlands, to formal areas such as the sunken garden next to Cannizaro House (now a hotel) and an Italian garden near the pond, expressing the changing face of garden design over the years.

The park is a joy at any time of year, thanks to the tireless efforts of the Friends of Cannizaro Park; it's particularly special in spring – when the rhododendrons, azaleas and magnolias are in bloom – and autumn, when the birch, maple and horse chestnut trees create a spectacular riot of colour.

Cannizaro Park, West Side Common, SW19 4UE (020-8545 3678; cannizaropark.com; Wimbledon tube; Mon-Fri 8am-dusk, Sat-Sun 9am-dusk).

Perched on the edge of Wimbledon Common, Cannizaro Park (Grade II* listed) was a private garden for some 300 years before opening to the public in 1949. The name Cannizaro dates from 1832 when Count St Antonio leased the house – he later succeeded to the dukedom of Cannizzaro in Sicily and left England to live with his mistress in Milan. His long-suffering wife Sophia retained her title as Duchess of Cannizzaro, and when she died in 1841 the estate was recorded under her name. Apart from losing a 'z', the name has stuck ever since.

Purchased by Wimbledon Corporation in 1948, the ravishing 35-acre park combines superb natural beauty with a unique collection of rare and exquisite trees and shrubs, including sassafras, camellia, rhododendron and other ericaceous plants. It's also noted for its rich wildlife. The

Clissold Park

Clissold Park is a much-loved public park in Stoke Newington extending to 55 acres, with a rich variety of trees and shrubs, a rose garden and an organic nature garden – even the benches are beautiful in Clissold Park. A Green Flag park since 2006, it also offers a wide range of facilities, including a playground, paddling pool, sports fields, bowling green, table tennis, basketball and tennis courts, plus a bandstand and a nice café. Animal attractions include an aviary, animal enclosures, a butterfly tunnel and terrapins in the lakes.

Named after former owner Reverend Augustus Clissold (1797-1882), the estate was purchased by the local authorities for a public park, which opened in 1889. Hackney Council and the Heritage Lottery Fund spent some £9m restoring the house and park to their former glory (completed in 2011).

Clissold Park, Green Lanes, N16 9HJ (020-8356 3000; hackney.gov.uk/clissold-park, clissoldpark.com; Manor House tube; daily 7.30am-dusk).

College Garden, Westminster Abbey

College Garden is the largest and most important of Westminster Abbey's gardens. Some 1,000 years ago it was the infirmary garden of the monastery, and it's said to be the oldest garden in England under continuous cultivation – records refer to a special medicinal herbarium

that was completed in 1306. While the original garden was principally an area in which to grow herbs, fruit and vegetables, it also provided convalescing monks with somewhere for relaxation and gentle exercise (and a final resting place, as part of the orchard was set aside as a cemetery). Hidden away to the south of the Abbey it's the perfect place to escape the crowds and you don't have to pay a Pope's ransom to enjoy it – entrance is free!

Westminster Abbey College Garden, 20 Dean's Yard, SW1P 3PA (020-7222 5152; westminster-abbey.org/about-the-abbey/history/abbey-gardens; Westminster tube; Tue-Thu 10am-4pm).

Culpeper Community Garden

Culpeper Community Garden is a green retreat in the midst of Islington's inner-city bustle; a beautiful and relaxing public space serving both as a park and an environmental community project. The garden is named after the famous 17th-century herbalist Nicholas Culpeper (1616-1654) and was created to provide somewhere children could learn to grow and care for plants and vegetables. Work began in 1982 to transform a derelict, rubbish-filled site into the lovely space you see today. Managed by and for local people, Culpeper employs part-time workers who develop projects with community groups and support volunteers, working with local children and schools. It's a peaceful place to spend some downtime, exploring the ponds and plants, and maybe enjoying a picnic.

Culpeper Community Garden, 1 Cloudesley Road, N1 0EJ (020-7833 3951; culpeper.org.uk; Angel tube; daily 10am-6pm).

Dulwich Park

Dulwich Park was previously part of the Manor of Dulwich, first mentioned in 967 and owned by Bermondsey Abbey until the Dissolution of the Monasteries in the 1530s. In the early 17th century, actor/impresario Edward Alleyn purchased the estate, and in 1885 the Dulwich Estate donated 'five fields' to the Metropolitan Board of Works for a public park. Opened in 1890, the park is considered the forerunner of modern country parks, and its 72 acres are packed with features, including a beautiful boating lake, several gardens and an expansive grassy area that's perfect for picnics. There's a plethora of historic and rare trees, including ancient oaks which mark its boundary, a bay laurel, swamp cypress, cypress oak and Indian bean.

Dulwich Park, College Road, Dulwich, SE21 7BQ (020-7525 2000; southwark.gov.uk/parks-and-open-spaces/parks/dulwich-park; North/West Dulwich rail; daily 7.30am-dusk).

Garden of St John's Lodge

The exquisite garden of St John's Lodge is the quintessential English garden, tucked away down a pergola-draped path on the edge of the Inner Circle in Regent's Park. A luxuriant oasis in the heart of the city, it offers excellent views of the imposing lodge, the first house to be built on Regent's Park in 1817-19, designed by John Raffield for Charles Augustus Tulk MP. It was one of the great villas envisaged by John Nash in his 'jewel in the crown' plan to transform the park and surrounding area in the 1800s; sadly, it's one of only a few villas that were actually built.

In 1892, a new garden 'fit for meditation' was designed at St John's Lodge for the third Marquess of Bute. Incorporating formal areas, a fountain pond, Doric temple, some fine statues, a stone portico and a partly sunken chapel, it reflects the Arts and Crafts ideas in vogue at the time and the revival of interest in the classical. The garden – which has been open to the public since 1928 and was renovated and redesigned in 1994 – is now completely separate from the Lodge and maintained by the Royal Parks.

In order to enjoy this haven of calm and beauty, you first have to find it! From the Inner Circle, proceed anti-clockwise past Chester Road, and some 200m further on you should find the (hidden) entrance gate to St John's Lodge Gardens on the right – if you pass the lodge you've gone too far!

Garden of St John's Lodge, Inner Circle, Regent's Park, NW1 4NX (0300-061 2300; landscapenotes.com/2013/03/22/st-johns-lodge-the-secret-garden; Regent's Park tube; daily 5am-dusk).

The Awakening

Golders Hill Park

A formal park which opened in 1898, Golders Hill Park adjoins the western part of Hampstead Heath but has been managed as a separate enclosed park by the City of London since 1989. The site was previously occupied by Golders Hill House, built in the 1760s by Charles Dingley but destroyed during the Second World War. The main characteristics of the park are a large expanse of grass dotted with specimen trees, a beautiful formal English flower garden, a Mediterranean garden, a walled garden, and a water garden with a number of ponds. The park's home to a free zoo, featuring coatis, kookaburras and ring-tailed lemurs, a butterfly house and a lovely café. It's also adjacent to the beautiful Hill Garden & Pergola (see page 110).

Golders Hill Park, West Heath Avenue, NW11 7QP (020-7332 3511; cityoflondon.gov.uk > green spaces > Hampstead Heath; Golders Green tube; daily 7.30am-dusk).

Highgate & Queen's Woods

Highgate and Queen's Woods (separated by Muswell Hill Road) are two large, well-preserved segments of the ancient Forest of Middlesex, which once covered much of London and is mentioned in the *Domesday Book* of 1086. In 1886, the City of London Corporation acquired Highgate Wood, then known as Gravelpit Wood, for public use. The wood covers 70 acres and is rich in oak, holly and hornbeam, plus the rare wild service tree – an indicator of ancient woodland. Queen's Wood (51 acres) is owned and managed by the borough of Haringey. It has a larger variety of flora and fauna than Highgate Wood, and is wilder with greater structural diversity and a denser shrub layer. Both woods have welcoming cafés.

Highgate & Queen's Woods, Muswell Hill Road, N10 3JN (020-8444 6129; Highgate Wood: cityoflondon.gov.uk > green spaces; Queen's Wood: haringey.gov.uk > parks & open spaces; Highgate tube; 7.30am-dusk).

Hill Garden & Pergola

The charming Hill Garden & Pergola are among the hidden delights of Hampstead Heath. The formal Arts and Crafts garden was created between 1906 and 1925 by celebrated landscape architect Thomas Mawson for the soap magnate Lord Leverhulme (1851-1925). It's situated at the rear of Inverforth House, formerly The Hill, which Leverhulme purchased in 1904 as his London residence. In 1925, The Hill was purchased by ship owner Andrew Weir, 1st Baron Inverforth, who lived there until his death in 1955. It was renamed Inverforth House in his honour when he left it to Manor House Hospital.

Mawson brought architectural treatment and formality to garden design, and the pergola and gardens are the best surviving examples of his work. The pergola was a magnificent Edwardian extravagance and the setting for garden parties and summer evening strolls. In late spring and early summer the raised, covered pergola – 800ft in length – is festooned with fragrant flowers, including jasmine, buddleia, sage, honeysuckle, vines, clematis, kiwi, potato vine, lavender and wisteria. Visit during the early evening and you may even see roosting long-eared bats.

In contrast to the wild decadence of the pergola, Hill Garden is beautifully manicured and designed; it's a little slice of paradise and a perfect antidote to the stresses of modern life, providing panoramic views over London.

Hill Garden & Pergola, Inverforth Close, off North End Way, NW3 7EX (020-7332 3322; cityoflondon.gov.uk > green spaces > Hampstead Heath > Golders Hill Park; Golders Green/Hampstead tube; daily 8.30am-dusk).

Inner & Middle Temple Gardens

You don't need to be a member of the legal profession to enjoy the glorious gardens of the Inner and the Middle Temple, two of the City's historic Inns of Court. The gardens, with their sweeping lawns, lavish floral displays and elegant courtyards, are thought to date back to the 12th century when the Knights Templar moved their base to this site

overlooking the Thames. The Inner Temple garden has unusual rare trees and charming woodland areas, while the award-winning Middle Temple gardens comprise a series of courtyards and one larger formal garden. Both attract plenty of wildlife, from bees and butterflies in the borders, to nesting birds such as robins, coal tits and blue tits.

Inner & Middle Temple Gardens, Middle Temple Lane, EC4Y 9AT (innertemple.org.uk, middletemple.org.uk; Temple tube; see websites for opening times).

Isabella Plantation

This stunning ornamental woodland garden was created within Richmond Park after the Second World War and covers an area of 42 acres south of Pen Ponds. Open to the public since 1953, it's managed organically, resulting in rich flora and fauna. It was Lord Sidmouth, then deputy ranger, who created the plantation in 1831, fencing it in to protect it from the park's deer and planting oak, beech and sweet chestnut trees. In spring there are camellias, magnolias, daffodils and bluebells, followed by azaleas and rhododendrons; in summer, Japanese irises and day lilies; while in autumn it's the turn of Guelder rose, rowan and spindle trees. During the winter months there are early camellias and rhododendrons, as well as mahonia, winter-flowering heathers and stinking hellebore.

Isabella Plantation, Richmond Park, TW10 5HS (0300-061 2200; royalparks.org.uk/parks/richmond-park; Richmond tube/rail; 7/7.30am-dusk).

Kensal Green Cemetery

Kensal Green is home to one of the capital's most beautiful and distinguished cemeteries. Opened in 1833, it's London's oldest, purpose-built public burial ground and was the first of the city's 'Magnificent Seven' Victorian cemeteries. Designed by John Griffith, it was laid out as an informal park with a number of formal features, such as manicured lawns, and a large number of specimen trees, including plane, cedar, chestnut, beech, lime, holm oak, poplar and yew. At 77 acres, Kensal Green is the largest and most opulent of London's cemeteries, containing some 250,000 graves. Today, large tracts have been set aside as nature and wildlife reserves, hence their sometimes overgrown and unkempt appearance, making it one of inner London's richest habitats for wildlife.

Kensal Green Cemetery, Harrow Road, W10 4RA (020-8969 0152; kensalgreencemetery.com; Kensal Green tube/rail; Mon-Sat 9am-5/6pm, Sun 10am-5/6pm).

Kyoto Garden, Holland Park

Holland Park is arguably London's most romantic public park, offering 54 acres of beautiful views, woodlands, gardens and sports facilities, plus peacocks, an ecology centre, some of London's best children's play facilities and a café – but the jewel in its crown is an immaculate Japanese garden. Created in 1991 and refurbished in 2001, Kyoto Garden is considered to be one of London's most tranquil spots, with a circular walkway, a koi carp pond with stepping stones, 15ft waterfall and seating areas. The pond is enclosed by elegant plantings of Japanese shrubs and trees – at their best in spring and autumn – which offer an ever-changing variety of vivid colours. It's the perfect place to 'escape' the city.

Kyoto Garden, Holland Park, Ilchester Place, W8 6LU (rbkc. gov.uk/leisure-and-culture/parks/holland-park; Kensington High Street/Notting Hill tube; daily 7.30am-dusk).

Morden Hall Park

Owned by the National Trust, Morden Hall Park encompasses over 125 acres of parkland in what was once rural Surrey. This tranquil former deer park is one of the few remaining estates that lined the River Wandle during its industrial heyday. As well as Morden Hall, it contains a stable yard, pretty Morden Cottage (situated in the rose garden) and many old farm buildings, plus a garden centre and café.

The Snuff Mill – one of the original Grade II listed mills – is used as an education centre. Visitors can see the conserved waterwheel that, until 1922, turned the massive millstones used to crush tobacco into fine powder for use as snuff and, behind it, the modern equivalent, an Archimedes screw hydro-electric turbine which generates electricity for the park's visitor centre.

The park sits on the flood plain of the River Wandle and consists of three main habitats: meadowland, marshland and woodland. Water lies at the heart of the park – with the river, mill ponds and a lake – and the lush wetlands, riverbanks and islands provide an ideal habitat for a variety of plants, insects, mammals (such as voles and pipistrelle bats) and, especially, birdlife. Herons, kingfishers, ducks and swans are regularly seen along the river, and there's a heron colony in the wetlands, which is also visited by a little egret. Rarer birds such as warblers shelter in the hedgerows, while woodpeckers and owls live in the woods.

Morden Hall Park, Morden Hall Road, SM4 5JD (020-8545 6850; nationaltrust.org.uk/morden-hall-park; Morden tube; daily dawn-dusk).

Mount Street Gardens

Mount Street Gardens is an unexpected oasis in Mayfair, laid out on the site of an early Georgian cemetery. It originally served as the burial ground for St George's Hanover Square, which had no adjacent churchyard, but the burial

ground closed in 1854 and, like many urban cemeteries, was later converted into a public garden. The gardens were laid out in 1889 with plants, paths and a small fountain, and have changed little since. Planting in the gardens includes mature London plane trees and a variety of smaller trees, shrubs and flowerbeds; the buildings that enclose the gardens create a microclimate which allows a number of rare trees, such as Australian silver wattle and a Canary Islands date palm, to flourish. An abundance of birdlife and welcoming benches make this a charming place to relax.

Mount Street Gardens, Mount Street, W1K 2TH (020-7641 2390; westminster.gov.uk/my-parks/parks/mount-street-gardens; Green Park/Bond Street tube; daily 8am-dusk).

Nunhead Cemetery

Consecrated in 1840, Nunhead Cemetery – named after the Old Nun's Head Tavern on nearby Nunhead Green – is the second-largest of London's 'Magnificent Seven' Victorian cemeteries. Its 52 acres were laid out by James Bunstone Bunning on former farmland, with curving paths and planting which took advantage of its elevated site. The cemetery's history, architecture and stunning views make it a fascinating place to visit, with many magnificent monuments erected in memory of the most prominent citizens of the day. Much of the cemetery is mysterious and overgrown, which many see as fundamental to its charm, with weathered gravestones, tumbling statuary poking through extravagant overgrowth and weed-choked paths. Not surprisingly, it's a haven for flora and fauna and a local nature reserve.

Nunhead Cemetery, Linden Grove, SE15 3LP (020-7732 9535; southwark.gov.uk/parks-and-open-spaces/parks/nunhead-cemetery, fonc.org.uk; Nunhead rail; 8.30am-dusk).

Phoenix Garden

This little oasis is the last remaining of Covent Garden's seven community gardens, and one of the West End's best-kept secrets. Founded in 1984, it's maintained by volunteers

and funded by donations. Tucked away behind the Phoenix Theatre – the entrance is in St Giles Passage – the award-winning garden arose phoenix-like on the site of a row of Georgian houses destroyed by a bomb in 1940. The less-than-ideal urban growing conditions have been no obstacle to a flourishing display of flowers, grasses, shrubs and trees, including rowan, willow, walnut and ginkgo. There's a rockery and fish pond, benches (with quirky inscriptions) and a play area – it's a living garden with heart and soul.

Phoenix Garden, 21 Stacey Street, WC2H 8DG (phoenixgarden.org; Tottenham Court Road tube; Mon-Fri noon-3pm).

Postman's Park

A short distance north of St Paul's Cathedral is one of the City of London's most interesting small parks, best known as the site of a poignant memorial. Postman's Park – the name reflects its popularity with workers from the nearby Post Office headquarters – stands on the old burial ground of St Botolph's Aldersgate and is a peaceful refuge. In 1900 it became the site of the Memorial to Heroic Self Sacrifice, the brainchild of artist George Frederic Watts (1817-1904), where over 50 plaques tell the tales of noble altruism – those commemorated died rescuing people from burning buildings, sinking ships and runaway horses, among other disasters. It's an inspiring tribute to 'ordinary' people.

Postman's Park, King Edward Street, EC1A 7BT (020-7374 4127; cityoflondon.gov.uk > things to do > green spaces > city gardens; St Paul's tube; daily 8am-dusk).

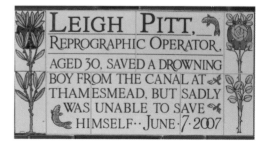

LEIGH PITT, REPROGRAPHIC OPERATOR, AGED 30, SAVED A DROWNING BOY FROM THE CANAL AT THAMESMEAD, BUT SADLY WAS UNABLE TO SAVE HIMSELF··· JUNE·7·2007

Queen Mary's Gardens

Tucked away in the Inner Circle of Regent's Park, Queen Mary's Gardens – named after the wife of George V – were laid out in 1932 on a site originally used as a plant nursery and later leased to the Royal Botanic Society. Some of the original pear trees that supplied fruit to the London market in the early 19th century survive. The gardens contain London's largest and best formal rose garden, a honey-pot for garden lovers (and bees) in spring and summer, when tens of thousands of plants are in bloom and the scent is intoxicating.

The famous rose garden contains over 400 different varieties in separate and mixed beds, and a total of some 30,000 rose plants. In addition there are around 30,000 other plants, including the national collection of delphiniums and 9,000 begonias, all laid out in landscaped beds surrounded by a ring of pillars covered in climbers and ramblers.

The Inner Circle also has the beautiful Triton Fountain, designed by William McMillan RA and donated in 1950 in memory of the artist Sigismund Goetze (1866-1939) by his wife Constance, plus an Open Air Theatre (openairtheatre.com) and a lovely café. It's hard to imagine a more peaceful place for a picnic.

Queen Mary's Gardens, Inner Circle, Regent's Park, NW1 4NU (0300-061 2000; royalparks.org.uk/parks/the-regents-park; Regent's Park tube; daily dawn-dusk).

Triton Fountain

Ravenscourt Park

This beautiful 32-acre public park and garden in west London was once the grounds of 17th-century Ravenscourt House (only the stable block remains and is now the park's café). The park combines attractive

landscaping with a range of wildlife habitats. Its crowning glory is the magical, scented walled garden, secreted in the northeast corner of the park, laid out in a traditional Victorian symmetrical design, with rose beds and arches and exotic herbaceous beds featuring yuccas, giant poppies, irises and gunnera. It's bordered below the wall with shrubs, while scented plants such as lavender and honeysuckle make it a real treat for the nose as well as the eyes. The garden is a wonderful, Zen-like retreat, with benches and bowers.

Ravenscourt Park, Ravenscourt Road, W6 0UL (020-8748 3020; lbhf.gov.uk/arts-and-parks/parks-and-open-spaces/ravenscourt-park; Ravenscourt Park tube; daily 7.30am-dusk).

St Dunstan-in-the-East Garden

The 12th-century church of St Dunstan-in-the-East was largely destroyed in the Blitz of 1941, although a tower and steeple added in the late 17th century by Sir Christopher Wren survived intact. The Corporation of London acquired the Grade I listed ruins, which were incorporated into a garden opened in 1971. Today, St Dunstan's is one of the City's loveliest gardens and a welcome retreat from the surrounding bustle. Visitors can enjoy a huge variety of plants that wend their way around the ruins; the walls and majestic windows have been draped and decorated with Virginia creeper and ornamental vine, which turn crimson in the autumn. A magical spot.

St Dunstan-in-the-East Garden, St Dunstan's Hill, EC3R 5DD (020-7332 3505; cityoflondon.gov.uk > green spaces > city gardens; Monument tube; daily 8am-dusk).

St Mary's Secret Garden

St Mary's Secret Garden is named after the church of St Mary's Haggerston, built by John Nash in 1827 but destroyed in the Second World War. Created in the '90s (named St Mary's Secret Garden in 2003), it's a tiny sanctuary – just 0.7 acre – divided into four areas: natural woodland with a pond, a food growing area, a sensory

garden and herbaceous borders. Organic principles are used to encourage wildlife and biodiversity, with the emphasis on social and therapeutic gardening. St Mary's offers horticultural therapy for those with mental health issues, terminal illnesses, and learning and physical disabilities. It's very much a community garden, but visitors are welcome – a beautiful spot in which to enjoy a few minutes' peace and quiet.

St Mary's Secret Garden, 50 Pearson Street, E2 8EL (020-7739 2965; stmaryssecretgarden.org.uk; Hoxton rail; Mon-Fri 9am-5pm, Sat 10am-1pm, closed Sun).

Tibetan Peace Garden

The Tibetan Peace Garden is located in Geraldine Mary Harmsworth Park in Southwark; it's a simple, poignant plea for peace, incongruously sited in the shadow of the Imperial War Museum. Commissioned by the Tibet Foundation and created by designer/sculptor Hamish Horsley, it was opened and consecrated in 1999 by His Holiness the Dalai Lama and honours one of his principal teachings: the need to create understanding between different cultures and establish places of peace and harmony in the world. The inner gardens are planted with herbs and plants from Tibet and the Himalayan region, while the pergola is covered with climbing plants, including jasmine, honeysuckle and scented roses. It's a spiritual, uplifting garden where visitors can enjoy some peace and reflection.

Tibetan Peace Garden, Geraldine Mary Harmsworth Park, St George's Road, SE1 6ER (tibet-foundation.org/page/peace_garden; Elephant & Castle tube; open 24 hours).

Victoria Park

Victoria Park is possibly the East End's best-loved park, covering 218 acres bordering parts of Bethnal Green, Hackney and Bow in the borough of Tower Hamlets. Opened in 1845, it's the oldest park in London created specifically for the public – hence its nickname the 'People's Park'. Designed by James Pennethorne, it's a stunning example of a formal London park, reminiscent of Nash's Regent's Park and deservedly Grade II listed. Although created as a place for people to breathe clean air, it's also a centre of horticultural excellence and boasts some delightful open parkland, wide carriageways, lakes, leisure gardens, ornate bridges over canals, and a wide variety of shrubs and trees, including copper beech and tulip. There's an excellent café, too (see page 44).

Victoria Park, Grove Road, E3 5SN (020-7364 2494; towerhamlets.gov.uk > Parks and open spaces; Mile End tube; daily 7am-dusk).

Waterlow Park

Situated in Highgate and bordered on two sides by Highgate Cemetery, Waterlow Park is named after its last private owner, Sir Sidney Waterlow (1822-1906), who gave his home, then called Lauderdale House, to London County Council in 1889 'for the enjoyment of Londoners' and as 'a garden for the gardenless'. The 29 acres of grounds became a public park and the house served for 70 years as a tearoom and

park-keepers' flats (it's now an arts and education centre with a peaceful café). Within the park there's a potpourri of formal terraced gardens – one of Britain's earliest examples – plus three ponds fed by natural springs, tree-lined walkways, mature shrub beds, herbaceous borders, ornamental bedding and verdant expanses of lawn.

Waterlow Park, Highgate Hill, N6 5HD (020-7974 5633; waterlowpark.org.uk; Archway tube; daily dawn-dusk).

York House Gardens

Around the restored cascades, planting has been designed to harmonise with the statues, with greens, pinks and whites predominating. The gardens also contain some unusual specimen trees and shrubs, added to enliven the landscaping, including several types of magnolia, *cornus contraversa* (wedding cake tree) and tulip trees – along with a beautifully restored Japanese garden.

York House Gardens, Sion Road, TW1 3DD (08456-122660; richmond.gov.uk > parks and open spaces, yorkhousesociety.org.uk/gardens; Twickenham rail; daily dawn-dusk).

These fascinating gardens are the grounds of Grade II listed York House, a handsome 17th-century building that's now the HQ of the London borough of Richmond, situated on the banks of the Thames in west London. The gardens – as they are today – were commissioned by Sir Ratan Tata (1871-1918), a Parsee industrialist from Mumbai who purchased York House in 1906. Tata installed a group of striking statues of naked female figures in the gardens, representing the Oceanides (or sea nymphs) of Greek mythology; female charioteers in a shell chariot drawn by winged horses plunge through the water at the top of a cascade and pool, while other figures perch on rocks or clamber up them. Also Grade II listed, the sculptures are carved from Italian white Carrera marble and are thought to have come from the Roman studio of Orazio Andreoni at the end of the 19th century.

8.
Places of Worship

From great cathedrals to historic City churches, London offers a huge variety of magnificent places of worship across the city. All offer somewhere to pray, meditate, contemplate, reflect or think, or just a spot to snatch a few moments of peace and quiet. History, architecture, religious art and glorious music are other excellent reasons to seek out those featured in this chapter – many also have a café. Entry is free unless stated otherwise.

All Hallows by the Tower

This ancient, Grade I listed church overlooking the Tower of London is the city's oldest, established back in 675 by the Saxon Abbey at Barking; for many years it was (confusingly) known as All Hallows Barking. However, people have worshipped here since much earlier times and the church was built on the site of a Roman building, of which there's evidence in the crypt.

All Hallows was expanded and rebuilt several times between the 11th and 15th centuries, and its location by the Tower saw it used for the temporary burial of execution victims, including Thomas More, Bishop John Fisher and Archbishop Laud. The church survived the Great Fire of 1666, during which Samuel Pepys famously climbed its spire to watch the progress of the conflagration. But it didn't fare so well during the Second World War, when it suffered extensive bomb damage necessitating major reconstruction.

Treasures include three beautiful 15th-16th century wooden statues of saints, a fine baptismal font cover (1682) by Grinling Gibbons and a splendid collection of medieval brasses. Down in the Crypt Museum you can view part of a 2nd-century Roman pavement and artefacts discovered during excavations – while next door there's a café serving tasty British food (bywardkitchenandbar.com) and a quiet courtyard garden.

All Hallows by the Tower, Byward Street, EC3R 5BJ (020-7481 2928; allhallowsbythetower.org.uk; Tower Hill tube; Mon-Fri 8am-5/6pm, Sat-Sun 10am-5pm).

Brompton Oratory

The Church of the Immaculate Heart of Mary – popularly known as the Brompton/London Oratory – is a stunning Roman Catholic church in South Kensington, next to the Victoria and Albert Museum. It's the church of a community of priests called The Congregation of the Oratory of St Philip Neri (or Oratorians), founded by Neri in 16th-century Rome. The Oratory was designed by Herbert Gribble, who won a design competition at the age of just 28, and the unabashed Italian style and ebullient décor are entirely intentional. The result is a ravishing, unique church, particularly in its use of colour and structure. Impressive as the exterior is, it's the extraordinary interior – where Italian influence is at its greatest – that takes the breath away. The music is excellent, too – try to visit when one of its three choirs is performing.

Brompton Oratory, Brompton Road, SW7 2RP (020-7808 0900; bromptonoratory.co.uk; South Kensington tube; daily 6am-8pm).

Christ Church Spitalfields

The spectacular 18th-century Christ Church Spitalfields in East London was designed by Nicholas Hawksmoor (1661-1736), a pupil of Sir Christopher Wren and one of England's foremost architects. Built between 1714 and 1729, it's noted for the eloquence of its beautiful stonework, pleasing geometry and proportions. The church is the size of a small cathedral; inside its roof is as high as that of Exeter Cathedral, while its volume is half that of the nave of St Paul's. Lit by chandeliers, it's a grand but serene space. Just as Christ Church is the masterpiece of its architect, the organ installed in 1735 is

considered to be the finest work of Georgian England's best organ builder, Richard Bridge.

Christ Church Spitalfields, Commercial Street, E1 6LY (020-7377 6793; ccspits.org, christchurchspitalfields.org; Liverpool Street tube/rail; Mon-Fri 10am-4pm, Sun 1-4pm).

Holy Trinity Sloane Square

This ravishing Victorian Anglican parish church was designed by John Dando Sedding (1836-1891) and built in 1888-90 in a striking Arts and Crafts style – it's aptly dubbed the 'cathedral of the

Arts and Crafts movement'. Grade I listed, Holy Trinity was certainly conceived on a grand scale; it's the widest church in the capital, eclipsing even St Paul's Cathedral by nine inches. However, it's the internal fittings that make Holy Trinity stand out as one of the finest Victorian churches in England, featuring the work of leading sculptors and designers of the day, including F. W. Pomeroy, H. H. Armstead and Hamo Thornycroft. It also has some glorious stained glass, including the Great East Window, designed by Edward Burne-Jones and manufactured by (William) Morris & Co.

Holy Trinity Sloane Square, Sloane Street, SW1X 9BZ (020-7730 7270; holytrinitysloanesquare.co.uk; Sloane Square tube; daily ca. 7.30am-6pm).

St Bartholomew the Great

Named for one of the 12 Apostles, Great St Bart's (as it's sometimes called) is one of London's oldest churches, with a rich history and fascinating architecture… and yet is surprisingly little known. A priory church was first established here in 1123 – by Rahere, a former jester at Henry I's court – as part of a monastery of Augustinian canons, and the site has been in continuous use as a place of worship since at least 1143. The Grade I listed church survived the Great Fire and the Second World War, and boasts London's most significant Norman interior, with massive pillars, Romanesque arches and zig-zag moulding. It's a tranquil retreat from the City's busy streets and well worth visiting despite the admission fee (£5).

St Bartholomew the Great, West Smithfield, EC1A 9DS (020-7606 5171; greatstbarts.com; Barbican tube; Mon-Fri 8.30am-4/5pm, Sat 10.30-4pm, Sun 8.30-8pm; fee).

St Bride's Church

St Bride's is one of London's oldest churches, dating back at least to the 7th century when the Middle Saxons converted to Christianity – or even to the 6th century when followers of St Bridget may have founded the

church. There's a section of Roman pavement in the crypt. The current church (Grade I listed) is the eighth on the site and was built by Sir Christopher Wren from 1672 to replace the 11th-century Norman church destroyed in the Great Fire. It's a striking building, topped by Wren's tallest (tiered) spire at 226ft, said to have inspired the shape of modern wedding cakes. St Bride's is often referred to as the 'journalists' church', as it offered a sanctuary for journalists when Fleet Street was the home of the UK newspaper industry.

St Bride's Church, Fleet Street, EC4Y 8AU (020-7427 0133; stbrides.com; St Paul's tube; Mon-Fri 8am-6pm, Sat 10am-3.30pm, Sun 10am-6.30pm).

St Dunstan and All Saints

Located in Stepney, St Dunstan's is the mother church of London's East End, and also its oldest church – its foundation dates back to the 10th century. The existing building is the third on the site, constructed of Kentish ragstone, mainly in the 15th century, although the chancel dates from 200 years earlier. A porch and octagonal parish room were added in 1872. The church is noted for its peal of ten bells, which is mentioned in the nursery rhyme *Oranges and Lemons*: 'Pray, when will that be, say the bells of Stepney'. While the church is charming, it's the vast churchyard – 7 acres of peace and quiet – that help make St Dunstan's really special.

St Dunstan and All Saints, Stepney High Street, E1 0NR (020-7702 8685; stdunstanstepney.com; Limehouse rail/DLR; Mon-Fri 10am-4.30pm).

St Ethelburga the Virgin

St Ethelburga the Virgin is one of very few medieval churches still standing in the City of London, as most were destroyed in the Great Fire of 1666. Dedicated to St Ethelburga (d. 675), a

7th-century abbess of Barking, the church's foundation date is unknown but is thought to be around 1180, although it was first recorded in 1250. It was rebuilt around 1411 and a modest square bell turret was added in 1775. It's the smallest church in the City – just 17m long and 9m wide – and one of the most delightful.

Grade I listed, St Ethelburga's has an exquisite exterior and is the loveliest building on the street by far, providing quite a contrast in terms of style, size and age with its neighbouring structures, particularly the 'Gherkin' building located behind it on St Mary Axe. Having survived the Great Fire and only suffering minor damage during the Second World War, it was almost destroyed in 1993 when a huge IRA bomb exploded nearby, but has since been restored.

The church is now a Centre for Reconciliation and Peace (see website for information), and offers a haven of quietness and reflection in a hectic part of London more commonly dedicated to Mammon.

St Ethelburga the Virgin, 78 Bishopsgate, EC2N 4AG (020-7496 1610, stethelburgas.org, Bank tube, 1st/3rd Mon of the month, 11am-3pm, or by appointment).

St James's Piccadilly

A majestic Anglican parish church on Piccadilly, built of red brick with Portland stone dressings, St James's (Grade I listed) was designed by Sir Christopher Wren and consecrated in 1684. Of the many churches Wren designed, this was one of his favourites and he singled it out for special praise. The interior boasts a number of superb features, including a carved marble font and limewood reredos by Grinling Gibbons. The church was badly damaged during the Second World War but later restored, and has the bonus of Southwood Garden, created in 1946 as a garden of remembrance and a venue for outdoor sculpture exhibitions. The church also has an impressive music programme and hosts various markets in its courtyard (piccadilly-market.co.uk).

St James's Piccadilly, 197 Piccadilly, W1J 9LL (020-7734 4511; sjp.org.uk; Piccadilly Circus tube; daily 8am-6.30pm).

St Leonard's, Shoreditch

Dedicated to the patron saint of prisoners and the mentally ill, St Leonard's is an elegant church dating from around 1740, designed in Palladian style by George Dance the Elder, a pupil of Sir Christopher Wren.

Its most prominent feature is its soaring 198ft steeple, inspired

by Wren's magnificent spire on St Mary-le-Bow in Cheapside. Many original 18th-century fixtures remain, including the font, pulpit, communion table, clock, organ case and commandment boards. In the medieval period, St Leonard's was the original 'actors' church' and the final resting place of many prominent Tudor actors, including Richard Burbage, a leading player in many of Shakespeare's plays. And like several East End churches, it gets a mention in *Orange and Lemons*: 'When I grow rich, say the bells of Shoreditch'.

St Leonard's, Shoreditch, Shoreditch High Street, E1 6JN (shoreditchchurch.org.uk; Shoreditch High Street rail; Mon-Fri noon-2pm, Sun 9.30am-1.30pm, closed Sat, tours by arrangement).

St Luke's Church

St Luke's (Grade I listed, with Grade II listed gardens) was designed by John Savage and opened in Chelsea in 1825. Built of Bath stone with flying buttresses and Gothic perpendicular towers along the 60ft nave and to the eastern end, it was one of the first neo-Gothic churches in London.

Laid out in the traditional 18th-century manner of a preaching house, it had an enormous pulpit, pews everywhere and a diminutive altar (although redesigned in the late 19th century). The burial ground surrounding the church was converted into a public garden in 1881, and today the delightful gardens are known for their beautiful flower beds and trees (visit in spring when they're in blossom), providing a welcome retreat from Chelsea's teeming streets. There's also a pleasant café.

St Luke's Church, Sydney Street, SW3 6NH (020-7351 7365; chelseaparish.org; South Kensington tube; Mon-Fri 9am-4pm).

St Margaret's Church

Standing between Westminster Abbey and the Houses of Parliament, the original St Margaret's – dedicated to St Margaret of Antioch – was thought to have been built in the 11th century for local folk to worship (without disturbing the Abbey's monks!). It was rebuilt between 1482 and 1523 and there were further restorations in the 18th-20th centuries, although the structure remains essentially the same; the interior was restored and altered by Sir George Gilbert Scott in 1877. St Margaret's became the parish church of the Palace of Westminster in 1614, a connection that continues to this day and has led St Margaret's to be dubbed 'the parish church of the House of Commons'. A restful (and free) alternative to the visitor-choked Abbey.

St Margaret's Church, St Margaret Street, SW1P 3JX (020-7654 4840; westminster-abbey.org/st-margarets-church; Westminster tube; Mon-Fri 9.30am-3.30pm, Sat 9.30am-1.30pm, Sun 2.30-4.30pm).

St Mary Aldermary

The most recent incarnation of St Mary Aldermary is an ashlar-faced 17th-century Anglican church with a gorgeous interior, built by Sir Christopher Wren. But there has been a church on this site for over 900 years; its name is usually taken to mean that it's the oldest of the City churches dedicated to the Virgin Mary.

The previous building, dating from the 16th century – said to have been among the largest and finest of the City's churches – was badly damaged in the Great Fire of 1666 and was rebuilt by Wren and opened in 1682. Grade I listed, it's the only surviving Wren church in the City built in the Gothic style; it follows the Late Perpendicular lines of the previous church, incorporating the walls and foundations that remained after the fire. The interior, however, is stunningly original and the mouldings and unique plaster vaulting in the nave and aisles make it a joy to visit.

St Mary Aldermary was damaged in the Blitz, when its windows were shattered and plaster fell from the vaulting, but the building itself remained intact. It was restored in the '50s and has been sensitively repaired many times over the years, most recently in 2005. It's now the home of the Moot monastic community and their admirable Host café.

St Mary Aldermary, 69 Watling Street, EC4M 9BW (020-7248 9902; achurchnearyou.com/church/15388, moot.uk.net; Mansion House tube; Mon-Fri 7.15am-4.45pm).

St Mary-le-Bow

The church of St Mary-le-Bow (Grade I listed) has a long and turbulent history. It was built around 1080 by Lanfranc (1005-1089), William the Conqueror's Archbishop of Canterbury, as his London headquarters. The original church suffered fire, collapse and even damage from a tornado; it was destroyed in the Great Fire and rebuilt by Sir Christopher Wren between 1671 and 1680, then destroyed again during the Second World War and rebuilt in 1964. The 11th-century crypt beneath the church was the first arched crypt found in any church in London; the 'le-Bow' in the church's name derives from these arches. Today, St Mary-le-Bow is probably best known as the church of 'Bow bells' and it's said that only those born within earshot of its bells are entitled to call themselves true Cockneys. The church is host to the superb Café Below (see page 35).

St Mary-le-Bow, Cheapside, EC2V 6AU (020-7248 5139; stmarylebow.co.uk; Mansion House tube; Mon-Wed 7.30am-6pm, Thu 7.30am-6.30pm, Fri 7.30am-4pm).

St Marylebone

Grade I listed St Marylebone – after which the district of Marylebone is named – is one of London's most romantic churches. The fourth church to serve the parish, it was designed by Thomas Hardwicke and consecrated in 1817. In 1885, major alterations were made, including the removal of the upper galleries to reveal the full length of the windows, which resulted in the magnificent church you see today. St Marylebone has many historical links: Lord Byron was baptised here, as was Lord Nelson's daughter, Horatia; Charles and Samuel Wesley were both buried here. And the poet Robert Browning and Elizabeth Barrett were secretly married here in 1846 after exchanging 574 love letters – a grand passion which is commemorated by the Browning Chapel, added in 1949.

St Marylebone, 17 Marylebone Road, NW1 5LT (020-7935 7315; stmarylebone.org; Baker Street tube; Mon-Fri 9am-5pm, Sat 9am-4pm, Sun 8am-4pm).

St Stephen Walbrook

This elegant City church has a link with the past going right back to Roman times. In the 2nd century AD a temple of Mithras stood on the banks of the River Walbrook – a stream that ran from the City Wall near Moorfields to the Thames – and was replaced by a Saxon church between 700 and 980AD. The current church (the third to stand here) was built by Sir Christopher Wren between 1672 and 1680; its interior, which is crowned by a glorious 63ft high dome, is considered one of Wren's finest, if not *the* finest. The influential British scholar of art and architecture Sir Nikolaus Pevsner declared St Stephen to be one of England's ten most important buildings, so it certainly merits attention. Its peaceful ambience is appropriate considering that the Samaritans charity for people in crisis was founded here by the rector Rev. Chad Varah in 1953.

St Stephen Walbrook, 39 Walbrook, EC4N 8BN (020-7626 9000; ststephenwalbrook.net; Bank tube; Mon-Tue, Thu 10am-4pm, Wed 11am-3pm, Fri 10am-3.30pm).

Saint Vedast-alias-Foster

Located close to St Paul's Cathedral is the beautiful Anglican church of St Vedast-alias-Foster. Vedast was a 6th-century bishop of Arras in northern Gaul (France), whose name was gradually anglicised into St Foster. The first church on this spot was built before 1170 and was rebuilt in the early 16th century but badly damaged in the Great

Fire of 1666. It was rebuilt by Sir Christopher Wren in 1699, although the striking spire, which rises in three stages of diminishing size, wasn't added until 1712. Wren's graceful church was gutted by firebombs during the Blitz and rebuilt in the '50s with attractive stained glass windows. It also has a delightful tranquil courtyard, accessed via an anonymous alleyway.

Saint Vedast-alias-Foster, 4 Foster Lane, EC2V 6HH (020-7606 3998; vedast.org.uk; St Paul's tube; Mon-Fri 8am-5.30pm, Sat 11am-4pm).

Southwark Cathedral

Southwark Cathedral is one of London's most beautiful and historic churches, a place of worship for over 1,000 years and the mother church of the Anglican diocese of Southwark, although it has only been designated a cathedral since 1905. Strategically sited at the oldest crossing point of the tidal Thames, it has long been a place, not just of worship, but of hospitality and refuge.

There are unsubstantiated claims that a convent was founded on the site in 606AD and a monastery by St Swithun in the 9th century, although the site's first official mention is in the *Domesday Book* of 1086, as the 'minster' of Southwark. The current building is mainly Gothic, dating from 1220 to 1420, making it London's first Gothic church. A Norman arch from the 12th century survives in the north aisle of the nave. It isn't just the building that's special: the cathedral is also rich in internal interest, including an oak effigy of a knight dating from around 1275 and a wealth of memorials and monuments.

The churchyard is a tranquil haven on the busy south bank and a favourite lunch spot for visitors and the area's office workers, particularly the welcoming Refectory Café. It's also a popular venue for concerts and recitals – see the website for the programme of events.

Southwark Cathedral, London Bridge, SE1 9DA (020-7367 6700; cathedral.southwark.anglican.org; London Bridge tube/rail; Mon-Fri 9am-5pm, Sat 9.30am-6pm, Sun 12.30-6pm).

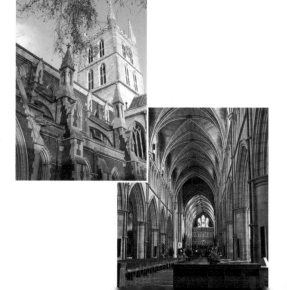

9.
Pubs & Bars

If you can avoid music and quiz nights, and sport on wide-screen TV, then pubs can be peaceful places. Our selection of pubs and bars includes those with shady gardens, private booths, discreet bar staff and laid-back dining rooms, where nothing should disturb you save for the clink of ice in a cocktail shaker or cutlery on china. However, bear in mind that a pub or bar that is deathly quiet all the time won't be in business for long...

American Bar

The American Bar on the Savoy Hotel's first floor evokes the roaring '20s, the so-called golden era of cocktails. It's an impressive venue – ranked 2nd in the world's 50 best bars 2018 by Drinks International – with understated Art Deco styling, elegant curves and Terry O'Neill photographic portraits on the walls, while a tuxedoed pianist plays American jazz to add to the ambience. *The Savoy Cocktail Book*, published by Savoy barman Harry Craddock in the '30s, remains the cocktail mixologist's bible, and the position of head bartender here is still one of the hospitality world's most prestigious appointments. The Savoy is also home to the equally glamorous Beaufort Bar.

American Bar, Savoy Hotel, 100 Strand, WC2R 0EU (020-7836 4343; fairmont.com/savoy-london/dining/americanbar; Charing Cross tube/rail; Mon-Sat 11.30am-midnight, Sun noon-midnight, £££).

Artesian Bar

Rated the world's best bar for many years by Drinks International, the Artesian is one of London's most sumptuous watering holes – a triumph of classic-meets-contemporary design – in one of the city's grandest 5-star hotels. Updated by the noted David Collins Studio, it blends Victorian opulence – marble bar, mirrors and embroidered napkins – with modern magnificence: purple, leather-effect upholstery, ornate wood panelling and an extravagant 'Chinese Chippendale' centrepiece, as the pagoda-like back bar is called. It isn't a cheap date, but neither is it ruinously expensive considering that it's one of the world's best bars.

Artesian Bar, Langham Hotel, 1C Portland Place, W1B 1JA (020-7636 1000; artesian-bar.co.uk; Oxford Circus tube; Mon-Sat 11am-2am, Sun 11am-midnight; ££-£££).

The Atlas

The Atlas may be a plain-looking pub in a Fulham backstreet, but appearances can be deceptive as it's a noteworthy gastropub. Despite this label, it isn't a trendy bar infested with yuppies but a friendly traditional local. The simple, spacious bar area – split into eating and drinking sections – has been renovated but retains original features such as glazed tiles, wood panelling and wall benches, stone fireplaces, and a melange of 'school'

chairs and well spaced tables. Outside there's an attractive walled garden for those all-too-infrequent sunny days, with an overhead awning and heaters for cooler evenings. A civilised and relatively peaceful place to enjoy good food, beer and wine.

The Atlas, 16 Seagrave Road, SW6 1RX (020-7385 9129; theatlaspub.co.uk; West Brompton tube; Mon-Sat noon-11pm, Sun noon-10.30pm; £-££).

The Avalon

Named after the mythical island at the heart of the legend of King Arthur, the Avalon is an attractive garden pub in South Clapham. The cavernous, lavishly-decorated dining room offers above-average pub grub – with gastro pretensions – serving free-range meat from its own farm (try the steaks and burgers) and sustainably-caught fish. The Avalon's pièce de résistance is its abundance of outside spaces, including a 'summer garden' complete with its own bar, a covered and heated courtyard and a heated front terrace. And there are plenty of corners in which to get away from it all, enjoy dinner à deux– or even catch up on work (there's free wifi).

The Avalon, 16 Balham Hill, SW12 9EB (020-8675 8613; theavalonlondon.com; Clapham South tube; Mon-Wed noon-11pm, Thu noon-midnight, Fri-Sat noon-1am, Sun noon-10.30pm; £-££).

Boot & Flogger

This looks like a pub and has a typically pubby name, but the Boot & Flogger in Southwark is actually a wine bar. Owned by Davy's Wine Merchants (est. 1870), it opened in 1964 – trading as a 'Free Vintner', a privilege granted by the Worshipful Company of Vintners (sadly abolished in 2005) – which may just make it London's first

proper wine bar. That said the atmosphere is redolent of a much earlier period, the wood panelling and leather armchairs suggesting the bonhomie of a gentlemen's club.

The substantial wine list includes more than 20 wines available by the glass, with prices starting at around £5 for a small (125ml) glass or £20 a bottle, and there's a fair choice of half bottles, too. If you're in the mood to celebrate, you can have a tankard of champagne! And if you're really pushing the boat out, Davy's list of fine wines contain some serious Bordeaux and Burgundy vintages. There's an interesting food menu, too, including meats hand-carved off the bone, award-winning steak, superfood salads and seasonal dishes, finishing with a substantial British cheese board and sticky puds.

The Boot & Flogger is a great place to unwind and is in one of London's most fascinating quarters. It's right opposite one of the city's more poignant historical sites, Cross Bones Graveyard, the resting place of over 15,000 Londoners (mostly women, many prostitutes) buried in unmarked graves on unconsecrated ground but remembered by floral tributes on the gate.

Boot & Flogger, 10-20 Redcross Way, SE1 1TA (020-7407 1184; davy.co.uk/wine-bar/boot-and-flogger; Borough tube; Mon 11am-10pm; Tue-Sat 11am-11pm; Sun noon-6pm; ££).

Buckingham Arms

A traditional Young's pub, the Buckingham Arms is a friendly and welcoming haven in St James's. It's an attractive Victorian pub dating from the early 19th century, with leather armchairs, a handsome mirrored back bar and an interesting side corridor with an elbow ledge for drinkers. The pub will appeal to fans of traditional, unpretentious venues serving well-kept ales – it's one of only two London pubs to appear in every edition of the CAMRA (Campaign for Real Ale) Good Beer Guide – and classic pub grub. It's located on one of London's more curiously named streets: Petty France comes from Petit France, as this area once had a community of French Huguenots.

Buckingham Arms, 62 Petty France, SW1H 9EU (020-7222 3386; buckinghamarms.com; St James's Park tube; Mon-Fri 11am-11pm, Sat 11am-9pm, Sun noon-5pm; £).

Churchill Bar & Terrace

A stylish cocktail bar located in the Hyatt Regency hotel, the Churchill offers a selection of inventive cocktails, homemade tonics, premium spirits, fine wines, a delicious bar menu – and even a cigar menu. This is as you would expect in a bar that pays deep homage to Sir Winston Churchill: original photographs and love letters between Sir Winston and his beloved wife Clementine adorn the walls, alongside pictures of their pets, Jock, Rufus, and Pig. There are shelves full of books (for clients to peruse), curated by Daunt Books, and a lovely heated terrace with a life-size bronze of the great man, where you can snuggle up with hot water bottles and blankets on cooler evenings. Winnie would approve!

Churchill Bar & Terrace, Hyatt Regency, 30 Portman Square, W1H 7BH (020-7299 2035; thechurchillbar.co.uk; Marble Arch tube; Mon-Sat noon-2am, Sun noon-midnight; ££).

Connaught Bar

The more famous of this landmark Mayfair hotel's two bars (the other is the Coburg), the Connaught Bar was ranked 5th in the world's 50 best bars in 2018. Designed by interior design guru David Collins, it's a dramatic Art Deco drinking den wrapped in leather, marble and metal, in a palette of lilac and pink, pistachio and silver. Cosy and understated, with subtle lighting and efficient service, cocktails are the speciality here – it's particularly noted for its perfect martinis, which are gently stirred, never shaken (sorry Mr Bond). This exceptional (if expensive) bar effortlessly manages to combine 21st-century style with considerable Old World charm, and you're made to feel really special by the friendly professional staff.

Connaught Bar, The Connaught, Carlos Place, W1K 2AL (020-7314 3419; the-connaught.co.uk/mayfair-bars/connaught-bar; Bond St tube; Mon-Sat 11am-1am, Sun 11am-midnight; £££).

Crocker's Folly

An opulent Victorian pub serving modern Lebanese cuisine and cocktails, Crocker's Folly (Grade II* listed) dates from the 1890s when Frank Crocker built The Crown Hotel to cash in on trade from the planned nearby terminus of the Great Central Railway in St John's Wood. No expense was spared, but unfortunately the railway's route was changed, the hotel was unsuccessful, and the

name was changed to Crocker's Folly in 1987. Today, the beautifully restored building is one of London's most stunning pubs. Don't miss the glorious Marble Room featuring 50 different kinds of marble, Romanesque columns and carved mahogany, while the Lord's Room (private dining area) has original high ceilings, a grand fireplace and a spectacular crystal chandelier. There's also a nice terrace.

Crocker's Folly, 24 Aberdeen Place, NW8 8JR (020-7289 9898; crockersfolly.com; Edgware Road tube; Mon-Thu, Sun noon-11pm, Fri-Sat noon-11.30pm; £-££).

Guildford Arms

A friendly local gastropub housed in a handsome Georgian building in Greenwich, the Guildford Arms has an elegant first floor restaurant, a private dining room and a stunning sunken garden. The ground floor 'pub' bar is relaxed and informal, offering a good selection of cask beers, lagers and wines, along with a menu featuring light bites, seasonal dishes and popular pub classics.

Food is definitely the focus here, particularly in the upstairs 'fine dining' restaurant, where chef-proprietor Guy Awford's modern British menu features the best of local and European seasonal produce. Star ingredients include Italian truffles, new-season English lamb, Scottish roast salmon and wild sea bass, and the set lunch (at £20 for three courses) is a steal. The carefully-selected wine list offers a wide selection from Europe and the New World, many available by the glass and carafe.

The Guildford's USP is its spectacular sunken garden which features both lawn and decked terrace areas, where white birch, tall grasses and kitchen herbs combine to create an oasis of calm. In summer it's the perfect place to relax with a jug of Pimm's or a chilled bottle of rosé, while tucking into delicious food from the barbeque.

Guildford Arms, 55 Guildford Grove, SE10 8JY (020-8691 6293; theguildfordarms.co.uk; Deptford Br DLR; Wed-Fri noon-3pm, 6-10pm, Sat noon-10pm, Sun noon-4pm, 5-9pm, closed Mon-Tue; £-££).

Hampshire Hog

This gastro pub is located in a quiet street in Hammersmith, although the calm and welcoming Hampshire Hog actually feels like a country pub. It's owned by Abigail Osborne and Tamsin Olivier, previously at the excellent Engineer pub in Primrose Hill, and styles itself a 'pub and pantry'. The pub puts an emphasis on food – it serves breakfast on weekdays and brunch at weekends, along with a scrumptious daily lunch

and dinner menu – while the pantry sells artisan produce and cook books. It's a handsome building, bright and spacious, with white walls, fancy mirrors and mismatched furniture, and outside there's the bonus of a large terrace and garden.

Hampshire Hog, 225-227 King Street, W6 9JT (020-8748 3391; thehampshirehog.com; Ravenscourt Park tube; Mon-Thu 8am-10pm, Fri 8am-11pm, Sat 10am-11pm, Sun 10am-6pm; £-££).

Island Queen

Situated on an Islington back street near the Regent's Canal, the Island Queen blends the theatrical Victorian gin palace with a laid-back colonial air. Built in 1851 – and remodelled in the 1880s – the pub retains many attractive original features, including its wood and glass frontage, mosaics, etched glass screens, high ceilings, mirrors painted with foliage and a curved island bar. More modern touches include comfy sofas, colourful rugs and dark wood furniture, which make for a cosy atmosphere. Add a wide choice of craft beers and superior pub grub, and you're in for a relaxing time. In summer, try to grab one of the outdoor tables at the front; the road is quiet, making it a good spot for an alfresco drink.

Island Queen, 87 Noel Road, N1 8HD (020-7354 8741; theislandqueenislington.co.uk; Angel tube; Sun-Thu noon-11.30pm, Fri-Sat noon-midnight; £-££).

Junction Tavern

A large corner establishment with an enviable reputation, the Junction Tavern caters equally to both beer aficionados and gourmets. It's a typical Victorian affair with high ceilings and elaborately carved dark wood, and a choice of places to sit, including the warm and friendly front bar area – with a stunning bar top and original fireplace – an airy conservatory, large heated garden terrace and award-winning beer garden. The daily changing menu offers modern British bistro fare, while weekend options include Saturday brunch and all-day Sunday lunch. There's a reasonably-priced, comprehensive wine list, with many available by the glass, plus a good choice of ales.

Junction Tavern, 101 Fortess Road, NW5 1AG (020-7485 9400; junctiontavern.co.uk; Tufnell Park tube or Kentish Town tube/rail; Mon-Thu 5-11pm, Fri-Sat noon-midnight, Sun noon-11pm, £).

Lobby Bar

The Lobby Bar at trendy One Aldwych – a classy, contemporary hotel located just south of Covent Garden, on the edge of the City – attracts both financial and creative types. It was named one of the top five hotel bars in the world by the *Sunday Telegraph* and is a place to take someone you want to impress. This ultra-stylish bar with pillars, floor-to-ceiling windows, striking artwork, huge flower displays and polished limestone floor is a treat for the eyes. Drinks comprise a range of well-made cocktails and an extensive choice of champagne, wine and beer, as well as an interesting bar menu, including sharing platters – something for everyone.

Lobby Bar, One Aldwych, WC2B 4BZ (020-7300 1070; onealdwych.com/food-drink/the-lobby-bar; Covent Garden tube; Mon-Fri 8am-midnight, Sat 9am-midnight, Sun 9am-10.30pm; ££).

The Mayflower

Tucked away on the Thames path in Rotherhithe, this 18th-century tavern has had several names over the years and only became the Mayflower in 1957 – a nod to the Pilgrim Fathers who set sail from nearby in 1620. It's a charming little pub with a black and white frontage and leaded windows, oak beams and wood panelling.

There's a dining room upstairs, while simpler fare is served in the bar, and there are barbecues on the jetty on summer weekends. The Mayflower attracts both locals and tourists to enjoy views of the Thames from its rear deck, which juts out over the river; blankets and hot water bottles are provided on chilly nights.

The Mayflower, 117 Rotherhithe Street, SE16 4NF (020-7237 4088; mayflowerpub.co.uk; Rotherhithe rail; Mon-Sat 11am-11pm, Sun noon-10.30pm; £).

The Old Ship

A relaxing riverside pub on Upper Mall, the Old Ship (dating from 1722) is a haven from hectic Hammersmith, enjoying a spectacular setting. This handsome, airy Young's pub has the feel of a boathouse, with its maritime-themed decor, a classy main bar/restaurant (with open fires in winter), and a balcony and terrace overlooking the Thames. The pub's fare includes cask-conditioned beers, full-bodied wines, indulgent brunch dishes and a seasonal British menu featuring the likes of treacle cured pork collar; baked honey and thyme Somerset camembert; 28-day-aged Angus sirloin steak; and smoked haddock, hot roast salmon, fennel and prawn pie. Well worth dropping anchor for.

The Old Ship, 25 Upper Mall, W6 9TD (020-8748 2593; oldshiphammersmith.co.uk; Ravenscourt Park/ Hammersmith tube; Mon-Thu 11am-11pm, Fri 11am-midnight, Sat 9am-midnight, Sun 9am-10.30pm; £-££).

Queens

Queens (aka The Queens Pub & Dining Room) is an opulent Victorian gastropub, originally built as a hotel in 1898, located a short distance from the Clock Tower in Crouch End. It has a large central bar with lots of cosy nooks and crannies, dark wood, stained glass windows and high ceilings, plus a decadent dining room with a striking ornate ceiling and open kitchen. And out back, there's a pretty garden oasis that's heated on chilly days.

Part of the highly-rated Food & Fuel group, the award-winning Queens offers a wide choice of well-kept beers and ales from small independent breweries, as well as an interesting list of over 20 wines, available by the bottle and glass, along with 'seasonal' cocktails. However, it's the delicious modern British cuisine that packs in the punters – and the friendly, professional service that keeps them coming back for more.

The menu changes daily and mixes pub favourites with more adventurous dishes, so you can tuck into roast salt marsh lamb, Cumberland sausages or beer-battered haddock or stretch yourself with Mediterranean mezze or moules marinière. It's good value for money and the menu also includes a smashing Sunday lunch.

Queens, 26 Broadway Parade, N8 9DE (020-8340 2031; foodandfuel.co.uk/our-pubs/the-queens-crouch-end; Crouch Hill/Hornsey rail; Sun-Thu noon-11pm, Fri-Sat noon-midnight; £).

Richard The First

Richard The First is a traditional boozer, perfect for those who aren't fussed about having dozens of beers from around the globe or cutting-edge wining and dining (though the food is tasty enough). A Young's pub, it's located on historic Royal Hill, one of Greenwich's loveliest roads, lined with Georgian houses and close to verdant Greenwich Park. It's housed in an 18th-century

building that used to contain two shops and has separate public and saloon bars, a division that's increasingly rare. To the rear is a stunning conservatory flooded in natural light, beyond which is a beautiful garden, a large open space bathed in sunshine in summer. It's a venue to cherish on a summer's day.

Richard The First, 52-54 Royal Hill, SE10 8RT (020-8692 2996; richardthefirst.co.uk; Greenwich DLR/rail; Mon-Sat noon to 11pm; Sun noon to 10.30pm; £).

Running Horse

Established in 1738, the Running Horse – a collaboration between James Chase of the award-winning Chase distillery and Dominic Jacobs, former bar director at Sketch – is the oldest public house in Mayfair. Restored in 2013, this charming, cosy pub features wood panelling, attractive fireplaces and lived-in furniture, including comfy sofas and armchairs, which give it the feel of a well-established traditional boozer (with some chic modern touches). The Running Horse prides itself on sourcing the finest British produce to create its regularly changing seasonal dishes, which include hand-chopped burger, lobster croissant and 'The Royal Half pies'. There are some decent ales on tap, including an Adnams lager and a couple of Meantime brews. Outstanding quality, if a tad expensive.

Running Horse, 50 Davies Street, W1K 5JE (020-7493 1275; Bond Street tube; therunninghorsemayfair.co.uk; Mon-Sat noon-midnight, Sun 11am-8pm; £-££).

Scarfes Bar

Named after the noted British satirical artist and cartoonist, Gerald Scarfe – whose work adorns the bar – the opulent and refined Scarfes Bar in the Rosewood Hotel is an atmospheric combination of drawing room, gentlemen's club and library, featuring a roaring fire in winter, low-key lighting, a beautiful long bar, cosy velvet armchairs and shelves overflowing with antique books. The bar specialises in whiskies – including over 200 single malts – and sloe gin, plus a few craft beers, although it's the creative and expertly-made cocktails that pull in the punters. Cool jazz and appetising bar snacks add to its soothing allure.

Scarfes Bar, Rosewood Hotel, 252 High Holborn, WC1V 7EN (020-3747 8670; scarfesbar.com; Holborn tube; Mon-Sat 4pm-1am, Sun 4pm-midnight; ££).

Wells Tavern

Close to Hampstead Heath, the Wells Tavern dates back to the early 18th century when folk visited Hampstead for its spas (or wells). It was a run-down boozer when, in 2003, it was rescued and transformed into today's eye-catching Georgian gem. An acclaimed 'pub-with-food', the Wells is a highlight of the Hampstead gastro scene, offering a diverse lunch and dinner menu, plus roasts on Sundays. Prices are at the top end for gastro fare, but not excessive for food of this quality. And it's a 'free' house so the range of beers

is extensive. The noisier ground floor has the bar and fireplace, plus bare tables, board games, dog bowls and squashy sofas. Upstairs is quieter with three very different dining rooms, or you can chill out on the terrace.

Wells Tavern, 30 Well Walk, NW3 1BX (020-7794 3785; thewellshampstead.co.uk; Hampstead tube; Mon-Sat noon-11pm, Sun noon-10.30pm; ££).

Ye Olde Cheshire Cheese

One of the City's must-see pubs located just off Fleet Street, Ye Olde Cheshire Cheese was already a century and a half old when it was rebuilt in 1667 after the previous year's Great Fire. Its atmospheric vaulted cellars are even older, and are thought to have belonged to a 13th-century Carmelite monastery that once occupied the site.

Now Grade II listed, it's an attractive, creaky warren of bars, full of little enclaves and hidey holes, especially cosy in winter when the coal fire is burning. It feels like a genuine history trip, and perhaps the long list of noted regulars (shown by plaques) has left its mark. It's probably the most illustrious who's who of drinkers of any London pub and includes (allegedly) Dr Johnson (who lived nearby), Sir Joshua Reynolds, Edward Gibbon, Charles Dickens (seemingly a regular at half of London's pubs – how did he find time to

write?), David Garrick, Thomas Carlyle, Alfred Lord Tennyson, WM Thackeray, Mark Twain, Theodore Roosevelt, Arthur Conan Doyle, GK Chesterton and WB Yeats, to name but a few.

The 'Cheese' is now a Sam Smith's pub, offering the brewery's usual range of well-priced ales and traditional pub fare. But however good the food and drink, it's the wonderful 17th-century atmosphere that keeps people coming back for more.

Ye Olde Cheshire Cheese, 145 Fleet Street, EC4A 2BU (020-7353 6170; Chancery Lane/Temple tube; Mon-Fri 11.30am-11pm, Sat noon-11pm, closed Sun; £).

10.
Shops & Markets

Shopping isn't just about clashing elbows at the sales or steering a trolley round the supermarket aisles. London is crammed with unique small shops, specialist retailers and fascinating markets, where shopping is a treat rather than a chore. The places featured in this chapter offer the ultimate in retail therapy – and it's unlikely you'll leave with empty hands or a heavy heart.

Beyond Retro

A store selling true vintage clothing – all goods started life as donations to charities – Beyond Retro opened their vast flagship superstore in Dalston in 2011. The Art Deco building was a Daks suiting factory in the late '20s and stood in for a Cuban cigar factory in the 2002 James Bond film *Die Another Day*. Its vaulted ceilings and vast floorplan have allowed Beyond Retro to create their most theatrical space yet, complete with innovative displays and quirky props – like the electric guitars on the fitting room walls. The well-edited collection of vintage and second-hand clothing (for men and women) gives it the air of a vintage department store – a relaxing place to browse – and the café continues the theme with vintage tea sets and old Singer sewing machines for tables.

Beyond Retro, 92-100 Stoke Newington Road, N16 7XB (020-7729 9001; beyondretro.com; Dalston Kingsland rail; Mon-Tue, Sat 10.30am-7pm, Wed-Fri 10.30am-8pm, Sun 11.30am-6pm).

Botanique Workshop

A florist with a difference, the Botanique Workshop combines blooms with handicrafts – and lets you get hands-on with flowers as well. Located in Clerkenwell's Exmouth Market, it's owned by imaginative Alice Howard who dreamed of creating a shop combining flowers, plants and gifts. Fresh bouquets are created in-house and delivered across the capital. There's also a collection of handcrafted products, including pots and vases, accessories (such as wire hair turbans made from gorgeous Liberty Print fabrics), jewellery, homeware and cards, either made in-house or sourced from like-minded independent British designers and makers. Botanique's workshops cover subjects from screen printing to sewing, as well as floristry skills, and are a delightful way to spend a few hours.

Botanique Workshop, 31 Exmouth Market, EC1R 4QL (020-3638 5621; botaniqueworkshop.com; Angel/Farringdon tube; Mon 10am-7.30pm, Tue-Sat 9am-7.30pm, Sun 11am-6pm).

Cabbages & Frocks

The delightfully named Cabbages & Frocks market is held on Saturdays in the cobbled yard of St Marylebone Parish Church (see page 130) in Marylebone Village. It's one of London's loveliest neighbourhoods with a wealth of interesting independent shops, cafés and restaurants. The market is foodie heaven, full of artisan and organic goodies, from olive oil and balsamic syrup to divine cupcakes and perfect patisserie, delicious cheeses and olives. If you're peckish, food stalls serve up Argentinian steak sandwiches, hog roast, sushi, organic crepes and much more. Non-food wares include handicrafts from local designers and cottage industries, including retro and vintage clothing, homeware, hand-blown glass and jewellery. A great place to browse.

Cabbages & Frocks Market, St Marylebone Parish Church Grounds, Marylebone High Street, W1U 5BA (020-7794 1636; cabbagesandfrocks.co.uk; Baker Street tube; Sat 11am-5pm, plus Christmas market).

Camden Passage Antiques Market

Camden Passage is like a little corner of London forgotten by time – an 18th-century, alleyway running along the back of Islington's Upper Street – but this cobblestoned backwater is a hotspot for antiques and collectibles. Here you'll find a multitude of stalls selling an eclectic mix of desirable things – vintage clothes, handbags, jewellery, silver, porcelain, glass

and assorted bric-a-brac – as well as a range of elegant Georgian antiques shops, pubs, cafés and restaurants. The antiques market is held on Wednesdays and Saturdays, although the larger shops also open on other days or by appointment. There's also a craft, gifts and food market on Sundays (10am-4pm).

Camden Passage Antiques Market, Camden Passage, N1 8EE (camdenpassageislington.co.uk; Angel tube; Wed & Sat, 6.30/7am-4/5pm).

Cass Art

The flagship store of Cass Art in Islington is the UK's largest art supply store, daubed over three floors of a former factory – some 7,500ft² of crafters' heaven. One floor is dedicated to painting and drawing, another to paper and canvas, while the lower ground floor is packed with kids' creative supplies and a large range of craft, printmaking and modelling materials. All the staff are artists and provide expert advice. The store contains a range of interactive spaces to make every visit a unique experience, along with a demonstration table where you can try out products, pick up tips and techniques, and attend workshops led by artists and suppliers. The store is also a community hub where you can sit and read, hold meetings and peruse the events board.

Cass Art, 66-67 Colebrooke Row, N1 8AB (020-7354 2999; cassart.co.uk; Angel tube; Mon-Wed, Fri 9.30am-7pm, Thu 9.30am-8pm, Sat 10am-7pm, Sun noon-6pm).

Columbia Road Flower Market

East London's most colourful street market, Columbia Road is the city's only dedicated flower market. It began in the 1800s as a food market but has evolved into the floral event you see today, when on Sundays the street is transformed into an oasis of foliage, cut flowers and plants – everything from trays of pansies to 10-foot banana trees. The market has been a must-visit attraction since the '80s, when it was revitalised by the increasing popularity of TV gardening programmes. However, Columbia Road offers much more than flowers and plants, and encompasses over 50 independent shops located in original Victorian buildings, as well as many excellent pubs, cafés and restaurants. It's a delightful place to spend a relaxing – and fragrant – Sunday.

Columbia Road Flower Market, Columbia Road, E2 7RG (020-7613 0876; columbiaroad.info; Hoxton rail; Sun 8am-3pm).

Connaught Village

Connaught Village is the Hyde Park Estate's luxury retail quarter, a quiet and charming oasis just a short stroll from Marble Arch and Hyde Park. It consists of a triangle of streets stretching from busy Edgware Road to artsy Bayswater,

and if you travel via gritty Edgware Road it's like entering a parallel universe: elegant Georgian and Victorian mews terraces, hanging flower baskets, neat streets and expensively dressed people. This leafy haven is home to an exclusive mix of independent retailers – luxury goods, artisan food, designer boutiques, etc. – as well as smart restaurants, sophisticated galleries and leading designers. Soak up the rarefied atmosphere and chill out over a coffee in Roni's Bagel Bakery at 12 Connaught Street.

Connaught Village, Connaught Street, W2 2AA (020-7287 9601; Connaught-village.co.uk; Marble Arch tube).

Couverture & The Garbstore

A cult, high-end designer fashion and homeware store in Notting Hill, Couverture & The Garbstore is actually two shops in one. On the ground floor and above is the Couverture take on womenswear, home and lifestyle – the collections include clothing and accessories, children's and baby-wear, toys, jewellery, home accessories, furniture and covetable vintage finds. Downstairs is The Garbstore for menswear, cutting-edge classic clothing, along with independent labels, vintage pieces and accessories. Overall, it's one of those stores where it's a pleasure to while away an hour browsing or just gawping at the exhibits and setting – more like a conceptual art space than a shop – even if you aren't planning to splash the cash.

Couverture & The Garbstore, 188 Kensington Park Road, W11 2ES (020-7229 2178; couvertureandthegarbstore.com; Ladbroke Grove tube; Mon-Sat 10am-6pm, Sun noon-5pm).

Design Centre

The Design Centre at Chelsea Harbour is a powerhouse of interior design, dedicated to inspire, inform and deliver the best in design, both for professionals and the general public. The Centre offers a unique shopping experience, with around 120 showrooms extending to over 90,000ft², showcasing over 600 of the world's most prestigious interior design brands – it's the largest collection of its kind in Europe and has been described by *Vanity Fair* as the 'interior design world's Mecca'. Synonymous with great design, it isn't surprising that every aspect of the Design Centre has been conceived to create the ultimate environment, with spectacular glass domes flooding the interior with natural light and sleek, curved glass balustrades.

From classic contemporary to cutting-edge cool all under one roof, the Design Centre brings together fabrics, wall coverings, furniture, lighting, accessories, kitchens, bathrooms, paint, outdoor living, curtain poles, hardware, tiles, carpets and much more. Many showrooms also offer a tailor-made approach for those seeking something bespoke. It's the perfect place to discover world-class talent, connect with influential designers, and get the inside track on high profile events and design lectures (see website for details).

There's also a design bookshop and a choice of three cool – and beautifully designed – cafés.

Design Centre, Chelsea Harbour, Lots Road, SW10 0XE (020-7225 9166; dcch.co.uk; Imperial Wharf rail; Mon-Fri 9.30am-5.30pm, closed weekends).

Floris

Founded in 1730 by Juan Famenias Floris (originally from Menorca), Floris is the oldest independent, family-owned perfumer in the world and still occupies its original premises in Mayfair. It's the only appointed perfumer to Her Majesty the Queen and was granted its first royal warrant by George IV in 1820, which was followed by 19 others. Its wide range of products are still developed in Jermyn Street by the in-house perfumer team and approved by Edward Bodenham, the Floris 'nose' and a 9th-generation member of the Floris family. Floris also creates bespoke perfumes, giving clients the opportunity to customise an existing scent. A treat for the nose and the soul.

Floris, 89 Jermyn Street, SW1Y 6JH (020-7747 3612; florislondon.com; Piccadilly Circus tube; Mon-Sat 9.30am-6.30pm, Sun 11.30am-5.30pm).

House of Hackney

Established in 2010 by husband and wife Javvy M Royle and Frieda Gormley, House of Hackney was founded as a label, first and foremost, although its flagship store in Shoreditch has become a destination for design aficionados. Its aim was 'to take the beige out of interiors', with an emphasis on quality, design and English heritage. The award-winning store stocks all the brand's products, from eiderdowns and furniture to lampshades and wallpaper. Javvy and Frieda are huge fans of the revered British textile designer William Morris and were approached in 2015 by the William Morris Gallery to reimagine Morris for a new generation. Not surprisingly, there are many echoes of Morris around the store, particularly in the glorious use of colour and pattern.

House of Hackney, 131 Shoreditch High Street, E1 6JE (020-7739 3901; houseofhackney.com; Shoreditch High Street rail/Liverpool Street tube; Mon-Sat 10am-7pm, Sun 11am-5pm).

James Smith & Sons

The home of the London umbrella – now famous around the world – James Smith has been making umbrellas, sticks and canes since 1830. A family-run business, it has been located in New Oxford Street since 1867. The store still has its original brass and mahogany shop front and hand-crafted interior fittings – made by the master craftsmen employed by the business – a nostalgic reminder of Victorian skills and values. James Smith has always thrived, thanks in part to London's unpredictable weather and its outstanding reputation and repair service. The devotion to quality is admirable, though prices are correspondingly high, so you may need to save up for a rainy day to buy an umbrella here!

James Smith & Sons, 53 New Oxford Street, WC1A 1BL (020-7836 4731; james-smith.co.uk; Tottenham Court Road tube; Mon-Fri 10/10.30am-5.45pm, Sat 10am-5.15pm, closed Sun).

Kensington Church Street

Kensington Church Street, running south from Notting Hill Gate to Kensington High Street, is one of London's most interesting shopping streets, particularly if you're a fan of antiques and collectibles. Originally a twisting lane joining two Roman roads from London – the north road led to Oxford, the southern one to Bath – today, the street (and its surrounds) is home to more than 60 antiques dealers. There's an abundance of quality independent shops offering fine art and antiques from the Tang dynasty to the Art Deco movement – visiting Kensington Church Street is like visiting an antiques fair that's open all year round. When you've had your fill of antiques, there are plenty of excellent cafés, restaurants and pubs nearby where you can relax and reflect on bargains gained (or missed).

Kensington Church Street, W8 (antiques-london.com; High Street Kensington/Notting Hill Gate tube).

Labour and Wait

Housed in an old Truman Brewery pub in trendy Shoreditch, Labour and Wait specialises in household goods. This may not sound too exciting, but it's a fascinating store, particularly if you care about good design and the future of the planet. The shop was established in 2000 by Rachel Wythe-Moran and Simon Watkins, who wanted to counter today's throwaway mentality with some old-fashioned quality and values. Their aim was to sell aesthetically pleasing but also functional products for everyday life, things that are good to look at and made to last.

Taking inspiration from Henry Wadsworth Longfellow's exhortation to 'Learn to Labour and to Wait' (from *A Psalm of Life*), they sourced goods that fit their ethos of good design, utility, quality and honesty, and have established themselves as one of London's leading independent shops. From hardware to clothing, kitchenware to bathroom accessories, stationery to gifts, L&W is very much in tune with the current 'war' on plastic. Some of its wares are new and innovative, while others are a nod to yesteryear, but all are ecologically-sound – from glass preserving jars and enamel kettles to string shopping bags. It all adds up to a collection of everyday classics that will mellow and improve with age.

Labour and Wait's calm and ordered atmosphere is an invitation to browse, and is jam-packed with treasures you never knew you couldn't live without…

Labour and Wait, 85 Redchurch Street, E2 7DJ (020-7729 6253; labourandwait.co.uk; Shoreditch High St rail; Mon-Fri 11am-6.30pm, Sat-Sun 11am-6pm).

Lamb's Conduit Street

Historic Bloomsbury's most elegant shopping street, Lamb's Conduit Street gets its unusual name from a wealthy Tudor gentleman, William Lambe, who built a conduit (or pipe) here to supply the city with spring water. The street became fashionable in the 19th century, when Charles Dickens lived in nearby Doughty Street, and remains so today. One of the things that sets the street apart from other shopping areas is the dearth of chains – this is a Starbucks-free zone – and plethora of independent businesses. Partly pedestrianised, the Street is home to a fine selection of boutiques and has, in particular, become a sophisticated hub for home-grown independent menswear designers, who have forsaken the crowds of Soho and Shoreditch to form a close-knit community in historic Bloomsbury. There are also two delightful Victorian pubs, the Lamb and Rugby Tavern.

Lamb's Conduit Street, Bloomsbury, WC1 (Russell Square tube).

Little Paris

Little Paris in Crouch End is a Francophile's delight – a treasure trove packed with an ever-changing eclectic mix of authentic vintage and antique furniture, curiosities and accessories sourced from *la belle France*. From contemporary design items, such as whimsical jewellery and Parisian scarves and hats, to off-beat vintage homeware, the shop's two rooms are packed with a mélange of crockery, film posters, authentic Tolix chairs and Jieldé lamps. Every month or so the owner, Hélène Allen, hops over the Channel to visit her favourite ateliers, *brocantes*, dealers and markets, to source fresh treasures. While not cheap, prices are reasonable and most items are in good condition. There's another outlet in Islington – you can check out Hélène's latest finds on her website.

Little Paris, 39 Park Road, N8 8TE (020-8340 9008; littleparisstore.com; Highgate tube/Crouch End rail; Mon 11am-6pm, Tue-Sat 10am-6pm, Sun 11am-5pm).

Neal's Yard

Remedies (NYR) followed in 1981 with its organic, plant-based health and beauty products, and now has over 50 stores across the UK and a growing presence throughout the world. Other celebrated outlets include Neal's Yard Bakery, Jacob the Angel (coffee shop) and the Wild Food Café.

You can easily while away a few hours here, with a massage in the NYR Therapy Rooms, a drink/snack in one of the cafés and a bit of people watching in this fascinating part of London.

Neal's Yard, Covent Garden, WC2H 9DP (Covent Garden tube).

Neal's Yard is a small alley and courtyard secreted in Covent Garden, tucked away between Shorts Gardens and Monmouth Street. Named after the 17th-century developer Thomas Neale (1641-1699) – who created the Seven Dials area where Neal's Yard is located – it's one of London's most colourful venues, where the buildings are painted in bright colours.

Neal's Yard became a retail destination in the late '70s when the area was derelict and rents were low (the old fruit and veg market had just upped sticks to south London and the new Covent Garden hadn't yet opened). First to move in was Nicholas Saunders, who opened a wholefood shop followed by a dairy, café and an apothecary specialising in alternative remedies and healing.

Neal's Yard Dairy opened in 1979, selling fresh cheeses and dairy produce, and now supplies restaurants throughout the UK. Neal's Yard

Monologue

A ravishing new contemporary design-concept store in buzzing Redchurch Street in Shoreditch (a few doors along from Labour and Wait, see page 155), Monologue was founded by interior designer Pavel Klimczak. With a focus on

conceptual design (with a Scandinavian slant), the store offers an exclusive selection of furniture, lighting, homeware, fashion accessories and stationery. Its collection encompasses marble and bright pops of colour in an ever-evolving design space, and offers a unique opportunity to discover the best of British and European

contemporary talent. Even if you can't afford to splash out several thousand pounds on a coffee table, it's still worth a visit to see the gorgeous wares on offer.

Monologue, 93 Redchurch Street, E2 7DP (020-7729 0400; monologuelondon.com; Shoreditch High Street rail; Mon-Sat 10.30am-6.30pm, closed Sun).

Mungo & Maud

The boutique of choice for posh pooches and cool cats, Mungo & Maud was the brainchild of Michael and Nicola Sacher who opened their store in Belgravia in 2005. The company styles itself 'dog & cat outfitters' and offers a range of design-led pets' accessories with a creative edge, made from natural materials such as wool, leather and linen. The collection is minimalist yet tactile, and ranges from hand-stitched leather collars to wooden feeding bowls, cotton beds and organic treats to an abundance of amusing accessories for the most discerning pets – all made to Mungo & Maud's own design. There are some nifty ideas for humans, too, including bags, books, gifts and walking accessories, such as indispensable poop bag pouches! It's the dog's …

Mungo & Maud, 79 Elizabeth Street, SW1W 9PJ (020-7467 0823; mungoandmaud.com; Sloane Square tube; Mon-Sat 10am-6pm, closed Sun).

Paper Mache Tiger

Opened in 2016, Paper Mache Tiger in Islington is a fashion and lifestyle boutique owned by Kyle Robinson (it's also the name and HQ of his fashion agency). Housed in a bright, spacious former pencil factory, with a high conservatory roof, the boutique offers an eclectic mix of in-the-know womenswear labels, arranged by colour palette rather than brand, and menswear offerings, enveloped by a veritable jungle of potted houseplants – banana trees, cheese plants, cacti and so forth – which are also for sale, as well as assorted 'trinkets' that Robinson picks up on work trips or unearths from vintage shops. Add a cosy coffee bar and it's clearly a place to linger.

Paper Mache Tiger, 26 Cross Street, N1 2BG (020-3490 7676; papermachetiger.com; Essex Road rail/Angel tube; Tue-Fri 10am-6pm, Sat 9am-6pm, Sun 11am-5pm, closed Mon).

Pentreath & Hall

Founded by architect and designer Ben Pentreath in partnership with friend Bridie Hall, this delightful small shop in the heart of Bloomsbury is a one-stop destination for home décor. It stocks well-designed and beautiful homeware, including china, glass, linens, furniture, pictures, candles, vases, lights, antiques, books and more, sourced from the UK, France, Belgium, Germany, Turkey and India, among other places. Pentreath & Hall is packed to the rafters with wonderful things not easily found elsewhere, from hand-blown glasses and colourful vases to stationery and art prints, kitchenware and lighting to cushions and candles. Utterly delightful.

Pentreath & Hall, 17 Rugby Street, WC1N 3QT (020-7430 2526; pentreath-hall.com; Russell Square tube; Mon-Sat 11am-6pm, closed Sun).

Pitfield London

A combination of homeware, design and lifestyle emporium, cool café and trendy art gallery, Pitfield epitomises the spirit of renewal and ingenuity in hip Hoxton. Occupying a huge, double-fronted, former office block with an edgy industrial feel, it's the retail outlet of celebrated interior designer Shaun Clarkson and business partner Paul Brewster, who've filled the bright open-plan space with an eclectic assortment of pieces acquired at home and abroad. Here you'll discover all manner of stylish furniture and home accessories, including colourful '70s seating, vintage glassware and lighting, exclusive Indian rugs, ultra-modern designer wallpaper, decorative objects, unique gifts and much more. The café is an extension of the Pitfield lifestyle and a good place to work, relax and socialise.

Pitfield London, 31-35 Pitfield Street, N1 6HB (020-7490 6852; pitfieldlondon.com; Old Street tube/rail; daily 10am-7pm).

Postcard Teas

Postcard Teas in Dering Street (just off Oxford Street) is at the forefront of the capital's renewed fascination with all things tea. The brainchild of owner Timothy d'Offay, his fascination for tea and tea culture was nurtured when he lived in Kyoto over 20 years ago, since when his passion has taken him throughout Asia. The tiny shop is home to rare teas from across the globe and specialises in what Tim calls 'small tea', i.e. tea from sustainable small family-owned farms, often just a few acres. Surprisingly, these small producers are responsible for around half the tea in Asia and for all the authentic examples of the famous teas of China, Japan, Korea, Taiwan and Vietnam. The shop runs tasting classes on Saturday mornings (10-11am), too.

Postcard Teas, 9 Dering Street, W1S 1AG (020-7629 3654; postcardteas.com; Bond Street tube; Mon-Sat 10.30am-6.30pm, closed Sun).

The Shop at Bluebird

One of London's most acclaimed concept stores, The Shop at Bluebird relocated its flagship store to Covent Garden in 2018 after 12 years on the King's Road in Chelsea. Its new home is a beautiful former coach house (Grade II listed) on Floral Street, with a cobbled courtyard, vaulted glass ceiling, soaring galleries, and original pulleys and beams, set against modern art installations and with a delightful bar and restaurant on the top floor.

Bluebird sources the best fashion, beauty and homeware pieces from around the world. Its owners' USP is only to stock pieces that they love and are excited to share. As such it stocks over 100 luxury and designer fashion brands – such as Victoria Beckham, Marni, Acne Studios and Alexander McQueen – alongside niche labels and emerging fashion talent like Forte Forte, Isa Arfen, Rixo and Ganni, interspersed with *objets*, ephemera, books, music and cult beauty brands.

Bluebird's team strives to create an eclectic experience that's both laid back and luxurious, where you can browse and buy the perfect outfit with the help of the store's personal shoppers. The new 15,000ft^2 luxury concept store is a one-stop shop and includes a number of in-store partners such as Blink Brow Bar, Fashion Illustration Gallery and Avery Perfume Gallery. And when you've finished splurging, you can treat yourself in the stylish bar/restaurant.

The Shop at Bluebird, Carriage Hall, 29 Floral Street, WC2E 9DP (020-7351 3873; theshopatbluebird.com; Covent Garden tube; Mon-Sat 10am-7pm, Sun noon-6pm).

Southbank Centre Book Market

One of London's best-kept secrets, the Southbank Centre Book Market on Queen's Walk (under Waterloo Bridge) is the city's only second-hand and antiquarian book market. Setting up their stalls daily, come rain or shine, the booksellers are London's answer to the *Bouquinistes* who ply their trade along the Seine in Paris – experts dealing in rare, old, hardback editions of the classics, manuscripts, poetry, art books, maps, photographs and prints, plus a wealth of second-hand paperbacks.

It's a great place to search for a rare first edition, but you don't have to be an avid collector to enjoy this book haven – it's for anyone who doesn't want (or cannot afford) to pay bookshop prices or is looking for an out-of-print title. If you're seeking a particular book you may find it here for a fraction of its original price – and usually in good condition.

Not as cheap as a car boot or charity shop, but a pleasant spot to browse and maybe pick up a pre-loved bargain. You can easily 'lose' a lunch hour or spend an entire Sunday morning examining the wares, and when you've had your fill of books you can pop into the Southbank Centre for a drink or meal.

Southbank Centre Book Market, beneath Waterloo Bridge/Queen's Walk, SE1 9PX (southbankcentre.co.uk/visit/shopping/markets/southbank-centre-book-market; Waterloo tube; daily early to 7pm).

11.
Spas & Relaxation

If your idea of peace and quiet includes warm bubbling water, scented oils, gentle massage and soothing meditation, then you'll find your nirvana in one of London's many spas and relaxation centres. A wonderful antidote to city life, we've chosen some of the very best, from self-indulgent day spas to Art Deco baths. Just grab a robe, clear your mind and… relax!

Ayurveda Pura

Ayurveda Pura is a luxurious day spa in Greenwich founded in 2003 by Dr Deepa Apté. The small, purpose-built spa facilities comprise four treatment rooms, two shower rooms, a yoga studio and a health café. It's also home to the Ayurveda Pura Academy which offers world-renowned training for therapists. Ayurveda – or 'science of life ('ayu' means life and 'veda' science) – is an Indian holistic medicine based on achieving physical and mental harmony with nature, and has been practised for over 5,000 years. The spa offers a wide range of beauty, Ayurvedic and holistic treatments, including sensual massage, detoxification and a number of unique healing therapies, plus waxing, threading and other beauty treatments.

Ayurveda Pura Health Spa & Beauty Centre, 48 Newton Lodge, Oval Square, Greenwich Millennium Village, West Parkside, North Greenwich, SE10 0BA (020-8312 8383; ayurvedapura.com; North Greenwich tube; £££).

Bamford Haybarn Spa

Located at the 5-star Berkeley, the Bamford Haybarn Spa is one of London's most luxurious day spas, with a marvellous rooftop pool, state-of-the-art gym, steam room and sauna. It boasts London's only heated rooftop pool, with panoramic views over Knightsbridge and Hyde Park, and a sliding roof that's open to the sky in fine weather. The spa follows a holistic approach to well-being and offers a vast range of treatments and packages, from standard beauty treatments such as eyebrow shaping, manicures and pedicures to massage, body wraps, waxing and Oskia facial treatments. There are also full- and half-day spa 'packages' available, including tailor-made treatments for pregnant women. Afterwards, you can swim and relax on the poolside sun-loungers or in the rooftop solarium courtyard with a glass of champagne. Sheer heaven!

Bamford Haybarn Spa, The Berkeley, Wilton Place, SW1X 7RL (020-7201 1699; the-berkeley.co.uk/health-club-and-spa; Knightsbridge/Hyde Park Corner tube; £££).

Chuan Body+Soul

Drawing on techniques from Traditional Chinese Medicine, the Chuan Body+Soul spa's treatments are tailor-made to revitalise and energise you from head to toe. Secreted away in a quiet corner of the 5-star Langham Hotel, the spa's exclusive facilities include a gym, steam rooms, Jacuzzi, Finnish and Himalayan rock salt saunas and a 16-metre swimming pool (with chandeliers!). The Chuan Harmony full-body massage releases tension through a combination of acupressure and various relaxation techniques, and is designed to balance the energy flow through the body, thereby inducing a deep sense of calm. If you book a treatment, make sure to allow an hour or two before or afterwards to make the most of the spa's other amenities.

Chuan Body+Soul, Langham Hotel, 2 Cavendish Place, W1B 3DE (020-7973 7550; chuanbodyandsoul.com/en/ london; Oxford Circus tube; £££).

COMO Shambhala

Small but perfectly formed, the COMO Shambhala spa at the Metropolitan Hotel in Mayfair is one of the city's best-kept secrets. Calm and warm with welcoming staff, the spa offers a huge range of beautifying treatments, such as facials and body scrubs and specialist therapies, ranging from a variety of massages – deep tissue, pre-natal, Indian head, Thai, Shiatsu,

etc. – to reflexology, acupuncture and more. The signature COMO Shambhala Massage uses specially blended oils to calm the senses and gently rejuvenate the body; it's an ideal massage for those looking to rebalance body and mind. For those in need of spiritual revitalisation, a session with one of COMO's visiting masters is sure to do the trick.

COMO Shambhala, COMO Metropolitan London, 19 Old Park Lane, W1K 1LB (020-7447 5750; comohotels.com; Hyde Park Corner tube; £££).

Elemis Day Spa

Located in a handsome period Mayfair townhouse in a courtyard just off New Bond Street (opposite the Mews restaurant and bar), the Elemis Day Spa is a haven of tranquillity. One of London's longest-established and best day spas, Elemis prides itself on providing clients with a sensory experience through its luxurious 'ritual' treatments, using its own renowned skin and body products. The waiting room has a contemporary Western vibe, with comfy chairs and inviting coffee-table books, enhanced by the wonderful aroma from Elemis' millennium candles. The black-clad therapists in their Eastern-tailored uniforms and bare feet are a foretaste of what's to come.

The revolutionary treatment menu includes everything from facials and massages to body scrubs and manicures. If you can't decide whether to treat yourself to a facial or a massage, then why not opt for the Total Face and Body Polish, which includes a full hour of pampering. Commencing with a warm foot cleanse, light body brushing and a luxurious balm massaged over the skin; followed by an exfoliating scrub that's left to sink into the skin as your body is wrapped in a cosy sarong; culminating in a prescribed anti-ageing facial that allows you to slip into a state of deep relaxation.

The ultimate spa packages last for up to four hours, but for those in a hurry there's the Speed Spa, where treatments last for just 30 minutes. There's also a range of treatments for men. Ultimate relaxation.

Elemis Day Spa, 2 Lancashire Court, W1S 1EX (020-7499 4995; elemis.com/house-of-elemis-london; Bond Street tube; £££).

ESPA Life Spa at Corinthia

ESPA Life at the 5-star Corinthia Hotel just off Whitehall is much more than 'simply' a spa – it describes itself as the 'Next Generation of Spa' and offers fitness, nutrition and complementary healthcare, in addition to luxury treatments. The grandeur of ESPA Life is breath-taking, and the futuristic lounge is a destination in itself, bathed in natural light and sculpted from dramatic Italian Calacatta white marble with champagne leather furniture and warm glowing fires. Spread over four floors, the spa has exclusive beauty and dining areas, treatment pods, discreet private spa suites, a state-of-the-art gym, nail studio and hair salon, plunge and jet pools, sauna, steam room, ice fountain and a stunning 9-metre swimming pool. The tough part is tearing yourself away from all this hedonism!

ESPA Life at Corinthia, Whitehall Place, SW1A 2BD (020-7321 3050; espalifeatcorinthia.com; Charing Cross/ Embankment tube; £££).

Evolve Wellness Centre

The Evolve Wellness Centre in South Kensington offers a variety of holistic treatments and classes, including yoga and Pilates, reflexology, chiropractic and Reiki, innovative lifestyle workshops, and a variety of courses for the body, mind and spirit. Whether your target is fitness, weight loss, reducing stress or improving your well-being, Evolve can provide you with the tools to build a healthier life. It's the brainchild of former ballerina and choreographer Corinne Blum and entrepreneur Adrian Kowal, both of whom are passionate about supporting people to grow, heal and develop. Evolve offers a choice of inexpensive membership packages and you can also sign up for workshops, courses – it's a centre of excellence for yoga – treatments and a dedicated weight-loss programme.

Evolve Wellness Centre, 10 Kendrick Mews, SW7 3HG (020-7581 4090; evolvewellnesscentre.com; South Kensington tube; £-££).

Floatworks

Drift away from the clamours of life in a floatation tank at Vauxhall's Floatworks, one of the world's leading floatation centres since 1993. Floatation REST (Restricted Environmental Stimulation Therapy) – also known as float therapy – involves floating in warm water that's super-saturated with Epsom salt, in a specially-designed tank (or slipper) resembling a large enclosed bathtub. The tank is designed to eliminate all outside distractions such as sight, sound and touch, and the salt content of the water helps you to defy gravity. Besides profound and deep relaxation, floatation is also used to treat a range of ailments including stress, insomnia, arthritis, high blood pressure, muscle aches and pains, and much more. The beneficial effects are cumulative, so the more often you float, the better you feel.

Floatworks, 17B St George Wharf, SW8 2LE (020-7357 0111; floatworks.com; Vauxhall tube; ££).

Indaba Yoga Studio

Indaba means 'gathering' and the Indaba Yoga Studio has indeed gathered a wide range of London's most talented teachers and built a community of yogis. Located in Marylebone, the Indaba Studio offers a rich array of yoga styles, providing classes for every ability and preference. There are classes for complete beginners, which concentrate on breathing, posture and alignment; dynamic and hot yoga if you want to break a sweat; experienced yoga if you want a challenge; and restorative yoga to calm you down. As well as classes, Indaba offers an extensive programme of workshops and courses, covering a wide range of creative and more traditional yoga styles, plus a myriad of treatments to help you relax and re-align. Prices are reasonable and the welcome is warm.

Indaba Yoga Studio, 18 Hayes Place, NW1 6UA (020-7724 9994; indabayoga.com; Marylebone tube/rail; ££).

Mandarin Oriental Spa

Recently renovated and enhanced, the luxurious Mandarin Oriental Spa in Knightsbridge offers a comprehensive menu of Chinese Traditional Medicine treatments and holistic body therapies – massages, scrubs, facials and more – using a range of products by Aromatherapy Associates, Sodashi and Linda Meredith. The spa has 13 treatment rooms and a new Oriental Suite for couples with massage beds and a Rasul water temple that combines the health enhancing properties of heat, steam and mud for a relaxing and skin conditioning treatment. Guests are encouraged to arrive at least 45 minutes before their appointment to enjoy the spa's heat and water facilities, which include an amethyst crystal steam room, sanarium (sauna with climate control), vitality pool and Zen colour therapy relaxation area.

Mandarin Oriental, 66 Knightsbridge, SW1X 7LA (020-7838 9888; mandarinoriental.com/london/hyde-park/luxury-spa; Knightsbridge tube; £££).

Marshall Street Baths & Spa

Marshall Street Baths in Soho were completed in 1931, although there have been public baths here since 1850. The stunning, marble-lined pool – 30m in length and recently restored to its former glory – is now part of the Marshall Street Leisure Centre and is a tranquil spot for an early-morning swim. In addition to the pool the centre is home to a fitness suite and the Everyone Spa, which includes an aroma steam room, sauna and a relaxation lounge. The spa offers a range of treats for face and body, including soothing facials, brown sugar body scrubs and reviving massages, as well as beauty treatments for men and women. Spa days allow you to combine a choice of treatments with some 'me' time in the spa.

Marshall Street Baths, Marshall Street Leisure Centre, 15 Marshall Street, W1F 7EL (020-7734 4325; everyonespa. com/our-venues/westminster-marshall-street; Oxford Circus tube; ££).

New Docklands Steam Baths

Hidden away in Canning Town in East London is an oasis of calm and relaxation, located in an unprepossessing industrial brick building next to the River Lea. However, don't be discouraged by appearances; what the NDSB lacks in opulence it more than makes up in health benefits and bang for your buck, with a range of treatments (for both men and women) designed to invigorate the skin, improve circulation and enhance your well-being.

Here you can enjoy the benefits of a traditional Turkish bath: sweat out the week's grime in the steam rooms, relax aching muscles and joints in the sauna, and chill out in an ice-cold plunge bath. If you're bold you can brave the Russian room and have your skin flogged to within an inch of its life in a schmeissing (a Jewish ritual carried out with a raffia brush), endure a venik treatment where you're 'beaten' with fragrant bundles of leafy silver birch or oak tree twigs, or be pummelled then gently massaged on one of the massage slabs.

Entry costs a maximum of £16 and you can simmer in the steam room or sauna for as long as you can stand the heat, while treatments are from £15 for 30 minutes or £30 for an hour. And when you're feeling rejuvenated you can grab a bite to eat or a drink in the café, watch some TV, access the free internet or have a nap in the comfortable lounge chairs.

New Docklands Steam Baths, 30A Stephenson Street, E16 4SA (020-7473 1454; newdocklands.co.uk; Star Lane DLR/ Canning Town tube; £).

The Spa in Dolphin Square

Dolphin Square in Pimlico is a vast iconic '30s apartment block, containing luxury apartments, a hotel, swimming pool, bar, brasserie, gymnasium, shopping arcade – and a marvellous spa. The spa has its own supply of mineral-rich water, drawn from an artesian well, with treatments revolving around the relaxing, cleansing and purifying experience of an authentic Moroccan hammam. Ideally, combine your hammam ritual with a *rhassoul* mud treatment to draw out toxins and impurities and/or a salt-infused steam bath to ease respiratory conditions and soothe aching joints. Add a massage and facial and finish off with delicious mint tea … or a glass of champagne. Magical!

The Spa in Dolphin Square, Dolphin Square, Chichester Street, SW1V 3LX (020-7798 6767; dolphinsquare.co.uk/spa; Pimlico tube; £££).

Spa Experience, York Hall

Located at York Hall Leisure Centre in Bethnal Green (dating from 1929 and best known for hosting prestigious boxing matches), Spa Experience (part of a chain of spas, formerly called Spa London) was the city's first public-sector day spa. What marks it out from most other spas in the capital is that it's affordable for 'normal' folk. Occupying York Hall's beautifully-restored former Turkish baths, the spa combines the best traditional thermal therapies with the latest modern spa treatments, plus a choice of over 50 health, beauty and relaxation treatments in partnership with leading brands such as Elemis. You can enjoy three hours in the spa for £26 and massages start from £38, so it's good for your wallet as well as your soul.

Spa Experience, York Hall Leisure Centre, Old Ford Road, E2 9PJ (020-8709 5845; spaexperience.org.uk/locations/bethnal-green; Bethnal Green tube/rail; £).

Ushvani Spa

Acclaimed as the UK's Best Day Spa by both *Tatler* and *Condé Nast Traveler*, Ushvani in Chelsea may well be London's most self-indulgent spa experience. It's located in an Edwardian building but the interior is pure Southeast Asia, from the wood-panelled and cream marble décor to the delicate aroma of ginger, nutmeg and pandan leaves that welcomes you in.

Ushvani specialises in traditional Southeast Asian treatments, such as Balinese massage and rituals using herbs, spices and essential oils. You're free to use the spa facilities, which include a hydrotherapeutic spa pool, themed showers and steam rooms. A nice touch is that you rarely see another client, so you feel like the pool and eucalyptus showers (the blasts of hot and cold water are designed to replicate a rain forest) are exclusively yours. Each treatment room has a different theme, for example the Asmara (Malay for 'love') Suite is used by couples, friends and relatives; the Blue Room is the men's treatment room; while the Sentosa Studio is for yoga, Pilates and meditation classes.

In keeping with Malaysian tradition, the spa treats men and women separately, so when necessary a screen is used to divide couples during treatments. The signature Malay massage and the Ushvani signature facial massage come highly recommended – only marginally cheaper than plastic surgery but much more enjoyable!

Ushvani Spa, 1 Cadogan Gardens, SW3 2RJ (020-7730 2888; ushvani.com; Sloane Square tube; £££).

12.
Miscellaneous

This chapter takes in palaces, houses, monasteries, docks, waterways, nature reserves, villages and streets, including one that pays homage to old Sicily. These are just a few of the special places that warrant a place in this book for the peaceful pleasures they offer, but don't quite fit into one of the previous chapters.

Carlyle's House

Once the home of Victorian polymath Thomas Carlyle and his wife Jane, this beautifully preserved Queen Anne house provides a fascinating peek at how middle-class, creative Victorians lived. The house remains much as it would have been in 1895 although the building is older, a typical terrace built in 1708. It's set in Cheyne Row, Chelsea, one of London's best preserved early 18th-century streets. Scotsman Thomas Carlyle (1795-1881) was one of the Victorian era's finest writers, said to have inspired Dickens, as well as a historian, philosopher and satirist, while his wife Jane was also a star of the literary scene. Inside the house, the attractive furniture, paintings, books and knickknacks paint a vivid picture of their domestic and work lives. Enlightening.

Carlyle's House, Cheyne Row, SW3 5HL (020-7352 7087; nationaltrust.org.uk/carlyles-house; Sloane Square/South Kensington tube; March to October, Wed-Sun 11am to 5pm – see website for exact dates; fee).

Charterhouse

Serene and peaceful Charterhouse – officially called Sutton's Hospital in Charterhouse – was originally a Carthusian monastery, founded in 1371 by Sir Walter de Mauny (Manny), one of Edward III's senior advisers. After the Dissolution of the Monasteries it became a private mansion and in 1611 was purchased by Thomas Sutton. He endowed a charitable foundation to educate boys, called Charterhouse School (now in Surrey), which later became an almshouse for gentlemen pensioners – as it remains to this day. Located in Smithfield, the beautiful Tudor Charterhouse (tours available, see website) is one of London's most captivating buildings and conveys a vivid impression of the rambling 16th-century mansions that once existed throughout the city. There's a lovely garden, too.

Charterhouse, Sutton's Hospital, Charterhouse Square, EC1M 6AN (020-7253 9503; thecharterhouse.org/tours; Barbican tube; fee).

Dennis Severs' House

One of London's most magical attractions, Dennis Severs' House is part exhibition, part installation; a work of fantasy, it's designed to recreate the atmosphere of the 18th and 19th centuries. The house was the brainchild of American artist Dennis Severs (1948-2000), who purchased it in the '70s, when the old Huguenot district of Spitalfields was run-down and little valued. Severs conjured up an imaginary family of Huguenot silk weavers, installed them in his house and, room by room, brought them back to life.

To do this, Severs filled the house with period fittings and furniture, as well as authentic smells and sounds, creating a genuine bygone atmosphere. Each of the ten rooms reflects a different era of the building's past and provides a snapshot of the life of the families who 'lived' here between 1724 and 1914.

A visit to the house is an essentially peaceful process. Visitors are asked to remain quiet while exploring this 'still-life drama' and touching objects isn't encouraged; it's the antithesis of a modern hands-on museum. You should also refrain from looking out of the windows to avoid being distracted by the 21st century outside. Tours take place on Sunday afternoons and Monday lunchtimes, and there are also evening candlelit tours (see website for bookings). Unusual, unsettling and enchanting!

Dennis Severs' House, 18 Folgate Street, Spitalfields, E1 6BX (020-7247 4013; dennissevershouse.co.uk; Liverpool Street tube; Sun noon-4pm, Mon noon-2pm, Mon, Wed, Fri 5-9pm; fee).

Dr Johnson's House

Biographer, editor, essayist, lexicographer, critic, moralist, poet ... Samuel Johnson (1709-1784) was possibly the most distinguished man of letters in English history, and his house reveals an absorbing glimpse of the great man. Built around 1700 and one of the few surviving residential properties of its vintage in the City of London, it was

Johnson's home and workplace between 1748 and 1759, where he compiled the first English dictionary. The elegant property has been restored to its original condition, with panelled rooms, period furniture, prints and portraits, while exhibits provide an interesting insight into Johnson's life and work. Don't miss the famous statue of Johnson's cat, Hodge, perched on a plinth in the square.

Dr Johnson's House, 17 Gough Square, EC4A 3DE (020-7353 3745; drjohnsonshouse.org; Chancery Lane tube; Mon-Sat 11am-5/5.30pm, closed Sun; fee).

Eltham Palace

Historic Eltham Palace (in southeast London) is an unexpected treat, combining one of England's best Art Deco interiors with some of the few significant remains of an English medieval royal palace. The palace was originally a moated manor house set in extensive parkland, before being given to Edward II in 1305 – it remained a royal residence until the 16th century and Henry VIII lived there as a young prince. The current building dates mainly from the '30s, when Sir Stephen and Lady Virginia Courtauld were granted a lease. They restored the Great Hall, which boasts England's third-largest hammer-beam roof, gave it a minstrels' gallery and incorporated it into a sumptuous home with a striking interior in a variety of Art Deco styles. Outside there are glorious gardens designed in a '30s style, plus a tea room and shop.

Eltham Palace, Court Yard, Eltham, SE9 5QE (020-8294 2548; english-heritage.org.uk/visit/places/eltham-palace-and-gardens; Eltham rail; see website for opening times; fee).

Hampstead Village

Hampstead is London's best-preserved Georgian village perched 440ft above sea level in northwest London. In the Middle Ages Londoners journeyed here to take the air and to escape the plague raging in the city below, and it became a fashionable spa town (Hampstead Wells) in the 1700s. It was the arrival of poets such as Keats and Shelley and artists Constable and Romney in the 18th and 19th centuries that helped establish Hampstead as a Bohemian artists' village; it has long been noted for its intellectual, liberal, artistic, musical and literary associations. Today, it's a ravishing urban village and a wonderful place to wander (despite the steep hills!), soak up some rich history, and admire the splendid architecture and views.

Hampstead Village, NW3 (hampsteadvillagelondon.com; Hampstead tube).

Little Venice & Regent's Canal

The term Little Venice is generally used to describe an area of around a square mile in London's Maida Vale district, roughly centred where the Paddington Arm of the Grand Union Canal meets the Regent's Canal. It's an unexpected haven of calm and beauty, comprising around ten tree-lined streets of graceful 17th-century stucco Regency mansions, many designed by the eminent architect John Nash. Regent's Canal (8.6mi/13.8km) was built in 1820 to link the Grand Union Canal with the Thames at Limehouse, and it meanders through the rich urban landscape of yesteryear, largely hidden behind high-rise buildings. Whether you stroll along the canal or take a trip on a narrow boat from Little Venice to Camden Lock, you'll discover one of London's best-kept secrets.

Little Venice, Maida Vale, W2 (en.wikipedia.org/wiki/little_ venice,_london; Paddington/Warwick Avenue tube).

Royal Hospital Chelsea

The Royal Hospital Chelsea is one of London's most historic and interesting buildings, housing some superb works of art and a small museum. It also serves a more practical purpose, as a retirement and nursing home for some 300 British soldiers (men and women) who are commonly referred to as 'Chelsea pensioners'. Indeed, the hospital was founded by Charles II and intended for the 'succour and relief of veterans broken by age and war'.

Designed by Sir Christopher Wren and completed in 1692, the beautiful, redbrick building is Grade I listed and regarded as London's second-loveliest façade on the Thames (after Greenwich). It's built around three courtyards – the centre one opens to the south, the side ones to the east and west – and remains almost unchanged, except for minor alterations by Robert Adam between 1765 and 1782, and the stables, which were added by Sir John Soane in 1814. Thus the Royal Hospital Chelsea is the work of three of Britain's finest architects. Even the stable block is regarded as an architectural gem, one of Soane's finest exteriors.

The attractive grounds – once the site of the popular 18th-century pleasure gardens, Ranelagh Gardens – are also open to the public and have hosted the celebrated Chelsea Flower Show (in May) since 1913.

Royal Hospital Chelsea, Royal Hospital Road, SW3 4SR (020-7881 5200; chelsea-pensioners.co.uk; Sloane Square tube; see website for opening hours and tours; free).

St Katharine Docks

Once one of the commercial docks that formed the Port of London, St Katharine Docks are situated just east of the Tower of London and Tower Bridge. The foundations can be traced back to the 10th century, although the docks opened in 1828 and at their peak in the '40s were the focal point for the world's largest concentration of portable wealth. Badly damaged in the Second World War, they never fully recovered and were among the first London docks to be closed in 1968. They were redeveloped in the '70s and today comprise offices, luxury apartments, a hotel, shops, food markets, bars, restaurants, cafés, a pub, yacht marina and other recreational facilities. It's an absorbing place to spend a relaxing hour or two.

St Katharine Docks, St Katharine's Way, E1 (020-7488 0555; skdocks.co.uk; Tower Hill tube/Tower Pier ferry).

Shad Thames

Soak up some of London's commercial history in Shad Thames, a street set back behind the converted warehouses that line the south bank of the Thames just east of Tower Bridge. In Victorian times Shad Thames (also used to describe the area surrounding the street) was home to London's largest warehouse complex, housing huge quantities of tea, coffee, spices and other commodities. After the Second

World War the area went into decline, with the last warehouse closing in 1972; regeneration began in the '80s and the picturesque warehouses – such as Butler's Wharf – were converted into luxury flats with restaurants, bars and shops on the ground floor. Look up to see one of Shad Thames' most striking features: the walkways which criss-cross the street high overhead and were used as bridges to roll barrels and transport goods between warehouses.

Shad Thames, Bermondsey, SE1 (en.wikipedia.org/wiki/shad_thames; Tower Hill/London Bridge tube).

Sicilian Avenue

This charming thoroughfare is one of London's most delightful streets. Screened at both ends by Corinthian columns in yellow terracotta, it has an authentic southern Italian vibe and feels as if it belongs in Palermo rather than Bloomsbury. The avenue was designed by Robert James Worley as a pedestrianised shopping street and completed in 1910. It was the inspiration of Herbrand Arthur Russell, 11th Duke of Bedford, who travelled to Sicily in the early 20th century and fell in love with the island. It's said he had a favourite street, on which the avenue's design is based; it boasts beautiful architecture with ornate carved stone façades and walkways edged in Sicilian black and white marble, while down the centre are lamp standards and parasols.

The original convex shop fronts are trimmed with dark wood and are home to a number of celebrated businesses, including Brooks & Brooks hairdressing, Stems' florists and several fashion boutiques. There's no shortage of places to eat and drink and in good weather the tables spill out into the street. The Spaghetti House is the most appropriate venue, but you can also choose between the Planet of the Grapes (wine bar),

the Onion Café and the Holborn Whippet pub. Magnifico!

Sicilian Ave, Holborn, WC1A 2QH (Holborn tube).

Southside House

Southside House is a handsome 17th-century property situated (appropriately) on the south side of Wimbledon Common. It was built in the late 1680s by Dutch architects for Robert Pennington, who shared Charles II's exile in Holland, and was later rebuilt in the William and Mary style. Behind the façade are the old rooms, still containing much of Pennington's original 17th-century furniture, and a superb collection of art and historical objects reflecting centuries of ownership.

Today, Southside House serves partly as a residence and partly a museum, hosting tour groups – including candlelit tours – and cultural events. Don't miss the glorious gardens with their wilderness, woodland, secret pathways and classical follies: an enchanting place to escape the stresses of modern life.

Southside House, 3-4 Woodhayes Road, Wimbledon, SW19 4RJ (020-8946 7643; southsidehouse.com; Wimbledon tube/rail; see website for tour information; fee).

Syon House & Park

Grade I listed Syon House and its 200-acre park comprise one of England's finest estates. The name derives from Syon Abbey, a medieval monastery of the Bridgettine Order founded in 1415 by Henry V and dissolved in 1539 by Henry VIII. In 1594, Henry Percy, 9th Earl of Northumberland, acquired Syon House through marriage and it has remained the London home of the Dukes of Northumberland ever since. The house was transformed in the 18th century by Robert Adam – it's acclaimed as his early English masterpiece and the finest surviving evidence of his revolutionary

use of colour – while the magnificent gardens and parkland are attributed to Lancelot 'Capability' Brown. You can always find a peaceful place in the gardens, which feature water meadows, majestic old trees and a marvellous 19th-century conservatory.

Syon House & Park, Brentford, TW8 8JF (020-8560 0882; syonpark.co.uk; Syon Lane rail; see website for opening times; fee).

Walthamstow Wetlands

A true oasis in busy north London, Walthamstow Wetlands is one of the largest urban wetland nature reserves in Europe, providing a home to many important wildlife species. The Wetlands – which encompass ten large reservoirs providing water to 3½ million homes – first opened to the general public in 2017 and have thirteen miles of footpaths and cycle tracks. It's designated a Site of Special Scientific Interest (SSSI) due to the reservoirs' international importance to breeding, migratory and wintering water birds and rare plants. In addition to a plethora of waterfowl, you may see soaring buzzards, peregrine falcons, kestrels and other birds of prey, while on warm summer evenings bats emerge at dusk from their roosting sites to feed on insects over the water. Magical.

Walthamstow Wetlands, 2 Forest Road, N17 9NH (walthamstowwetlands.com; Tottenham Hale tube; daily 9.30am-4pm; free).

Wapping High Street

Perched on the north side of the Thames, east of Tower Bridge, Wapping was a small village until 1805 when the area was transformed by the opening of the London Docks. It retained its strong maritime character well into the 20th century as a home to sailors, mastmakers, boat-builders, blockmakers, instrument-makers, victuallers, dockers and other trades associated with seafaring. The docks' decline began in the Second World War, when the area was devastated by German bombing, and when they closed in the '60s Wapping went into severe decline. Like many Thameside areas it's been the target of regeneration since the '80s, but Wapping seems immune to gentrification and retains much of its historic character. Today, it's a fascinating peaceful area to explore, its converted warehouses and historic houses seemingly untouched by time.

Wapping High Street, E1 (alondoninheritance.com/london-streets/wapping-high-street-and-wapping-wall; Tower Hill tube/Wapping rail/Shadwell DLR).

William Hogarth's House

Built between 1713 and 1717, Hogarth's House (Grade I listed) in Chiswick is the former country home of 18th-century English painter, engraver and satirist William Hogarth (1697-1764), who lived here with his wife, wife's cousin, mother-in-law and sister from 1749 until his death. It provided a quiet summer retreat from the bustle of city life around Hogarth's main house and studio, in what is now Leicester Square. While the area has since been swallowed up by London's urban sprawl, it remains a surprisingly tranquil spot.

It was opened to the public in 1904 – making it one of London's oldest house museums – by local landowner and Hogarth enthusiast, Lieutenant-Colonel Robert William Shipway. He donated the house to Middlesex County Council in 1907 and it's now managed by the London borough of Hounslow.

Two floors of the house are open to the public and include the most extensive collection of Hogarth's prints on permanent public display and some replica pieces of 18th-century furniture. The ground floor provides a general exhibition and discovery room, which includes digital presentations with an on-screen model of the whole of the building, as well as a small shop and exhibition gallery. Allow some time to visit the attractive walled garden, where there's a mulberry tree that's at least 300 years old.

William Hogarth's House, Hogarth Lane, Great West Road, W4 2QN (020-8994 6757; williamhogarthtrust.org. uk; Turnham Green tube; Tue-Sun noon-5pm, closed Mon; free).

The Marriage Contract

William Hogarth, self-portrait

London's Architectural Walks

Jim Watson, ISBN: 978-1-909282-85-8, 128 pages, softback, £9.99

London's Architectural Walks is a unique guide to the most celebrated landmark buildings in one of the world's major cities. In thirteen easy walks, it takes you on a fascinating journey through London's diverse architectural heritage with historical background and clear maps. Some of the capital's most beautiful parks are visited, plus palaces, theatres, museums and some surprising oddities. With the author's line and watercolour illustrations of all the city's significant buildings, London's Architectural Walks is an essential companion for anyone interested in the architecture that has shaped this great metropolis.

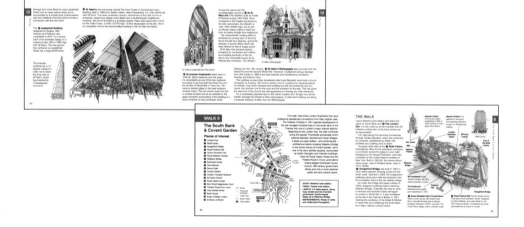

INDEX

London's Green Walks

ISBN: 978-1-909282-82-7, 192 pages, £9.99, David Hampshire

Green spaces cover almost 40 per cent of Greater London, ranging from magnificent royal parks and garden cemeteries, full of intrigue and history, to majestic ancient forests and barely tamed heathland; from elegant squares and formal country parks to enchanting 'secret' gardens. The 20 walks take in famous destinations, such as Hyde Park and Regent's Park, but also many smaller and lesser known – but no less beautiful – parks and gardens, all of which are free to explore.

London's Village Walks

ISBN: 978-1-909282-94-0, 192 pages, £9.99, David Hampshire

From its beginnings as a Roman trading port some 2,000 years ago, London has mushroomed into the metropolis we see today, swallowing up thousands of villages, hamlets and settlements in the process. Nevertheless, if you're seeking a village vibe you can still find it if you know where to look. Scratch beneath the surface of modern London and you'll find a rich tapestry of ancient villages, just waiting to be rediscovered.

London's Monumental Walks

ISBN: 978-1-909282-95-7, 192 pages, £9.99, David Hampshire

It isn't perhaps surprising that in a city as rich in history as London, there's a wealth of public monuments, statues and memorials: in fact London probably has more statues than any other world city. Its streets, squares, parks and gardens are crammed with monuments to kings and queens, military heroes, politicians and local worthies, artists and writers, and notables from every walk of life (plus a few that commemorate deeds and people perhaps best forgotten), along with a wealth of abstract and contemporary works of art.

LONDON'S HIDDEN SECRETS
ISBN: 978-1-907339-40-0
£10.95, 320 pages
Graeme Chesters

A guide to London's hidden and lesser-known sights that aren't found in standard guidebooks. Step beyond the chaos, clichés and queues of London's tourist-clogged attractions to its quirkier side.

Discover its loveliest ancient buildings, secret gardens, strangest museums, most atmospheric pubs, cutting-edge art and design, and much more: some 140 destinations in all corners of the city.

LONDON'S SECRET PLACES
ISBN: 978-1-907339-92-9
£10.95, 320 pages
Graeme Chesters & David Hampshire

London is one of the world's leading tourist destinations with a wealth of world-class attractions. These are covered in numerous excellent tourist guides and online, and need no introduction here. Not so well known are London's numerous smaller attractions, most of which are neglected by the throngs who descend upon the tourist-clogged major sights. What London's Secret Places does is seek out the city's lesser-known, but no less worthy, 'hidden' attractions.

LONDON'S SECRET WALKS
3rd Edition
ISBN: 978-1-909282-99-5
£10.95, 320 pages
Graeme Chesters

London is a great city for walking – whether for pleasure, exercise or simply to get from A to B. Despite the city's extensive public transport system, walking is often the quickest and most enjoyable way to get around – at least in the centre – and it's also free and healthy!

Many attractions are off the beaten track, away from the major thoroughfares and public transport hubs. This favours walking as the best way to explore them, as does the fact that London is a visually interesting city with a wealth of stimulating sights in every 'nook and cranny'.

LONDON'S HIDDEN CORNERS, LANES & SQUARES
ISBN: 978-1-909282-69-8
£9.95, 192 pages
David Hampshire

The inspiration for this book was the advice of writer and lexicographer Dr Samuel Johnson (1709-1784), who was something of an expert on London, to his friend and biographer James Boswell on the occasion of his trip to London in the 18th century, to 'survey its innumerable little lanes and courts'. In the 21st century these are less numerous than in Dr Johnson's time, so we've expanded his brief to include alleys, squares and yards, along with a number of mews, roads, streets and gardens.

see londons-secrets.com

LONDON'S CAFES COFFEE SHOPS & TEAROOMS
ISBN: 978-1-909282-80-3
£9.95, 192 pages
David Hampshire

This book is a celebration of London's flourishing independent cafés, coffee shops and tearooms – plus places serving afternoon tea and breakfast/brunch – all of which have enjoyed a renaissance in the last decade and done much to strengthen the city's position as one of the world's leading foodie destinations. With a copy of *London's Cafés, Coffee Shops & Tearooms* you'll never be lost for somewhere to enjoy a great cup of coffee or tea and some delicious food.

LONDON'S SECRETS: MUSEUMS & GALLERIES
ISBN: 978-1-907339-96-7
£10.95, 320 pages
Robbi Atilgan & David Hampshire

London is a treasure trove for museum fans and art lovers and one of the world's great art and cultural centres. The art scene is a lot like the city itself – diverse, vast, vibrant and in a constant state of flux – a cornucopia of traditional and cutting-edge, majestic and mundane, world-class and run-of-the-mill, bizarre and brilliant.

So, whether you're an art lover, culture vulture, history buff or just looking for something to entertain the family during the school holidays, you're bound to find inspiration in London.

LONDON'S SECRETS: PARKS & GARDENS
ISBN: 978-1-907339-95-0
£10.95, 320 pages
Robbi Atilgan & David Hampshire

London is one the world's greenest capital cities, with a wealth of places where you can relax and recharge your batteries. Britain is renowned for its parks and gardens, and nowhere has such beautiful and varied green spaces as London: magnificent royal parks, historic garden cemeteries, majestic ancient forests and woodlands, breathtaking formal country parks, expansive commons, charming small gardens, beautiful garden squares and enchanting 'secret' gardens.

LONDON'S SECRETS: PUBS & BARS
ISBN: 978-1-907339-93-6
£10.95, 320 pages
Graeme Chesters

British pubs and bars are world famous for their bonhomie, great atmosphere, good food and fine ales. Nowhere is this more so than in London, which has a plethora of watering holes of all shapes and sizes: classic historic boozers and trendy style bars; traditional riverside inns and luxurious cocktail bars; enticing wine bars and brew pubs; mouth-watering gastro pubs and brasseries; welcoming gay bars and raucous music venues. This book highlights over 250 of the best.

see londons-secrets.com

London's Waterside Walks

ISBN: 978-1-909282-96-4, 192 pages, softback, £9.99
David Hampshire, published Spring 2019

Most people are familiar with London's River Thames, but the city has much more to offer when it comes to waterways, including a wealth of canals, minor rivers (most are tributaries of the Thames), former docklands, lakes and reservoirs. *London's Waterside Walks* takes you along 21 of the city's lesser-known, hidden waterways.

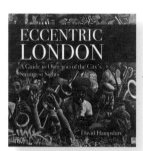

Eccentric London, 2nd edition

ISBN: 978-1-909282-98-8, 192 pages, softback, £9.99
David Hampshire, published Summer 2019

The British are noted for their eccentricities and London is no exception, with an abundance of bizarre and curious places and stories. *Eccentric London* explores over 300 of the city's more unusual places and sights that often fail to register on the radar of both visitors and residents alike.

London Escapes

ISBN: 978-1-909282-97-1, 192 pages, softback, £9.99
David Hampshire, published Autumn 2019

Although London offers a wealth of attractions, sometimes you just want to escape the city's constant hustle and bustle and visit somewhere with a gentler, slower pace of life. *London Escapes* offers over 50 days out, from historical towns and lovely villages to magnificent stately homes and gardens; beautiful, nostalgic seaside resorts and beaches to spectacular parks and nature reserves.

see citybooks.co